"Personal growth requires that we create healthy boundaries for our internal world, just as we are to do in our interpersonal relationships. When the various parts of our soul are connected and integrated, the result is that we heal, relate, and function at the highest levels. Alison Cook and Kimberly Miller have written a very helpful, engaging, and practical book on how to accomplish this process."

—Dr. John Townsend, *New York Times* bestselling author
of *Boundaries* and founder of the Townsend Institute

"*Boundaries for Your Soul* spoke to me in echoes of already-known, yet-not-fully-applied truths, as well as with sweet new understandings. For both those familiar with Jesus' inner healing and those new to the process, there is real help here. I plan to review the material often for myself, and share it with others."

—Elisa Morgan, author of *The Beauty of Broken*
and *The Prayer Coin*, cohost of *Discover the Word*,
and president emerita of MOPS International

"Is there a spirit-led self within you that emanates love and can lead your inner and outer life? Is it possible for you to love your inner enemies in the same way that Jesus extolled you to love your outer ones? In this beautifully-written book, Cook and Miller not only show you how to do that but also make a strong case that doing so creates enormous inner transformation and peace, turning former enemies into valuable allies. I am thrilled with the way they have translated my work for a Christian audience and believe this book is an extremely important contribution to our culture's healing."

—Richard C. Schwartz, PhD, developer of the Internal
Family Systems Model of psychotherapy

"Before we can realize an integrated life—a flourishing life—we must imagine it. We live in a world that often feels drained of the capacity as individuals, let alone as a culture, to imagine the life of an undivided heart, of an integrated soul. Into this world Miller and Cook step—nimbly, generously, and with great kindness. With *Boundaries for Your Soul* they offer us a wellspring of desperately longed-for imagery and actions that provide the opportunity for real change in real time and space. For all of those parts of us that have been waiting our entire lives to hear the call to come home and take their proper place and purpose of healing, wholeness, and creativity, I cannot think of a better place to start."

—Curt Thompson, MD, psychiatrist, speaker, and author
of *Anatomy of the Soul* and *The Soul of Shame*

"The Internal Family Systems model is a trusted method of psychotherapy that seeks to bring emotional growth by differentiating between the many complex parts of our personalities. *Boundaries for Your Soul* delivers the good news that we don't have to be controlled by our strong emotions. This thoughtful book is a rigorously compassionate, biblically-informed manual that can help you discover your true self in the choppy waters of life's ever-changing circumstances."

—Sandra McCracken, songwriter and musician

"Living with *overwhelm*—internal and external—is among life's most relentless and wearisome realities. Far too often the chaos without matches the cacophony within. With the courage to delve into the oft unruly and misunderstood realm of the soul, Kimberly Miller and Alison Cook point our divergent parts to Christ Jesus' invitation to his followers: 'Come unto me . . .' Here is a treatise that gracefully weaves together theory and Scripture, personal experiences with professional insights, and the wisdom of social scientists with the power of the Holy Spirit into one accessible tome. Miller and Cook have given us a gift."

—Kanyere Eaton, MSW, MDiv, senior pastor of
Fellowship Covenant Church, Bronx, NY

"Compelling yet accessible insights on a timely issue: our need to befriend the inner stranger. Our personal mental, spiritual, and emotional health depends on this kind of knowledge—and the health and common good of our society require that we examine our own inner landscape, searching for the clues that will enable us to resist coldness of heart. By gaining insight into our broken inner lives, we grow in empathy and love for those we naturally regard as strangers or enemies. Cook and Miller have given us a valuable tool to assist us in this important self-work."

—Bruce Herman, MFA, painter, creator of *Ordinary Saints* project, and author of *Through Your Eyes*

"What an accomplishment! When we have dissonance within our souls, our hearts crave harmony and wholeness. This groundbreaking book on boundaries helps us manage our emotions, improve our minds, and enrich our relationships. Everyone needs this!"

—June Hunt, founder, CEO, and CSO (chief servant officer) of Hope for the Heart and author of *The Answer to Anger* and *Counseling Through Your Bible Handbook*

"It was the apostle Paul who first floated the idea that the very hardest parts of being 'us'—or what he called 'thorns in the flesh'—have the unexpected potential to become our allies. It is through our thorns, Paul wrote, that the power and grace of God are most vividly manifested in our lives. In this helpful volume, Miller and Cook have done a great job of showing us how God can repurpose potentially destructive 'thorns' for good, including anger, fear, sadness, and guilt, so that we can become the best versions of ourselves. I hope this book is a help to you. It certainly was to me."

—Scott Sauls, senior pastor of Christ Presbyterian Church, Nashville, TN, and author of *Jesus Outside the Lines*, *Befriend*, and *From Weakness to Strength*

"Living in the freedom of an integrated life with God is a refreshing priority. This includes transforming the inner garden of the soul, even the weeds. Thanks to Miller and Cook, we now have in our hands this gentle, transformational journey that leads us graciously into healthy internal boundaries of Spirit-led self-leadership."

—Dr. Stephen Macchia, founder and president of Leadership Transformations, Inc. and author of *Becoming a Healthy Church*, *Crafting a Rule of Life*, and *Broken and Whole*

"Our culture often eschews boundaries and limits in the name of freedom, success, or power. Yet people without boundaries bring damage on themselves and others. And in the process they sabotage the very freedom, success, and power they want. Miller and Cook provide an accessible path to understanding why boundaries are hard and how we can grow through integrating them into our lives. I continually found myself saying, 'Thank you for these questions. Thank you for this insight. Thank you for giving names to the fault lines in the soul and the landmines in relationships.' If you are interested in transformation and seeing people change, this book is a must-read."

—Adele Ahlberg Calhoun, pastor of Spiritual Formation, Highrock Church, Arlington, MA, retreat speaker, Enneagram trainer, and author of *Spiritual Disciplines Handbook* and *Invitations from God*

"Using a psychological lens to refract the complexities and conflicts of the soul, Miller and Cook offer a Christian perspective as a resource to provide awareness, insight, and guidance for anyone seeking to integrate their painful and conflicting thoughts and feelings and achieve internal harmony. This is a worthy challenge and theirs is a remarkable achievement. We highly recommend this book to anyone seeking inner peace and joy, and that is a lot of people!"

—Harville Hendrix, PhD and Helen LaKelly Hunt, PhD, founders of Imago Relationship Therapy and *New York Times* bestselling authors of *Getting the Love You Want* and *Making Marriage Simple*

"In *Boundaries for Your Soul*, the authors have given us a great gift that will help people gain greater self awareness and new-found self-control over those unruly thoughts and feelings that threaten to derail our life and relationships."

—Leslie Vernick, relationship coach, speaker, and author of *The Emotionally Destructive Relationship* and *The Emotionally Destructive Marriage*

BOUNDARIES
FOR
YOUR SOUL

BOUNDARIES
FOR
YOUR SOUL

How to Turn Your Overwhelming
Thoughts and Feelings into Your Greatest Allies

**ALISON COOK, PhD, AND
KIMBERLY MILLER, MTh, LMFT**

NELSON
BOOKS

An Imprint of Thomas Nelson

Published in Nashville, Tennessee, by Nelson Books, an imprint of Thomas Nelson. Nelson Books and Thomas Nelson are registered trademarks of HarperCollins Christian Publishing, Inc.

The authors are represented by Ambassador Literary Agency, Nashville, TN.

Thomas Nelson titles may be purchased in bulk for educational, business, fund-raising, or sales promotional use. For information, please email SpecialMarkets@ThomasNelson.com.

Unless otherwise noted, Scripture quotations are taken from the Holy Bible, New International Version®, NIV®. Copyright © 1973, 1978, 1984, 2011 by Biblica, Inc.® Used by permission of Zondervan. All rights reserved worldwide. www.Zondervan.com. The "NIV" and "New International Version" are trademarks registered in the United States Patent and Trademark Office by Biblica, Inc.®

Scripture quotations marked AMP are from the Amplified® Bible. Copyright © 1954, 1958, 1962, 1964, 1965, 1987 by The Lockman Foundation. Used by permission. (www.Lockman.org)

Scripture quotations marked ESV are from the ESV® Bible (The Holy Bible, English Standard Version®). Copyright © 2001 by Crossway, a publishing ministry of Good News Publishers. Used by permission. All rights reserved.

Scripture quotations marked KJV are from the King James Version. Public domain.

Scripture quotations marked THE MESSAGE are from *The Message*. Copyright © by Eugene H. Peterson 1993, 1994, 1995, 1996, 2000, 2001, 2002. Used by permission of NavPress. All rights reserved. Represented by Tyndale House Publishers, Inc.

Scripture quotations marked NASB are from the New American Standard Bible®. Copyright © 1960, 1962, 1963, 1968, 1971, 1972, 1973, 1975, 1977, 1995 by The Lockman Foundation. Used by permission. (www.Lockman.org)

Scripture quotations marked NIRV are from the Holy Bible, New International Reader's Version®, NIrV®. Copyright ©1995, 1996, 1998, 2014 by Biblica, Inc.® Used by permission of Zondervan. All rights reserved worldwide. www.Zondervan.com. The "NIrV" and "New International Reader's Version" are trademarks registered in the United States Patent and Trademark Office by Biblica, Inc.®

Scripture quotations marked NLT are from the Holy Bible, New Living Translation. © 1996, 2004, 2007, 2013, 2015 by Tyndale House Foundation. Used by permission of Tyndale House Publishers, Inc., Carol Stream, Illinois 60188. All rights reserved.

Scripture quotations marked WEB are from the World English Bible™. Public domain.

ISBN 978-1-4002-0161-7 (TP)

ISBN 978-1-4002-0162-4 (eBook)

Library of Congress Control Number: 2018932497

Printed in the United States of America

23 24 25 26 27 LBC 27 26 25 24 23

To Joe and Ken,
for believing in and encouraging us

CONTENTS

CONTENTS

INTRODUCTION

WE KNOW A man who had it all. He was handsome, winsome, and gifted with many talents. When still in his youth, he became a powerful and famous leader. He was blessed with a large family and the respect of all who knew him. Most important of all, he had a genuine passion for God. He was devoted to prayer and worship, and he spent years building a reputation for integrity and success.

And yet, in time, this remarkable man yielded to unruly impulses that overtook him. It began when he noticed a beautiful woman and couldn't get her out of his mind. In a weak moment, he pursued her and slept with her, even though he knew she was married. Soon, she conceived his child. Fearing for his reputation, he searched for ways to conceal what he had done. When his attempts failed, he completely lost his moral bearings and arranged for the woman's husband to be killed. This conflicted man wanted to live a life of integrity, but instead tragically ended up doing many things he knew he shouldn't do—actions that hurt others and himself as well.

You may know this man too. His name is King David, and he's one of history's great heroes. He liberated Jerusalem from the Canaanites, brought the ark of the covenant—God's holy dwelling place—back to its rightful home, and united Israel's northern and southern kingdoms under his rule. He penned worship poetry and danced before the Lord with humble abandon. The Bible calls him "a man after [God's] own heart" (1 Sam. 13:14). But by David's own admission, his heart was divided. Although he had many virtues, his story reveals that parts of his soul were far from God, marred by pride, manipulation, murder, and deceit.

It makes you wonder, *what was David's problem?*

Many people would agree that David crossed a boundary when he sent for Bathsheba, the object of his desire and the daughter of one of his closest friends.[1] She and Uriah, her husband, had a sacred covenant, and David tore right through it. But before crossing Bathsheba and Uriah's boundary, didn't David first have a problem *within*—a problem with his own desire? Though a mighty warrior, David had been losing the battle for his soul. This internal boundary problem led to unnecessary pain and sorrow. And though we may not all have concubines and plot to kill their husbands, as David did, we can all be overtaken by extreme thoughts and feelings at times.

❧

Since the 1970s, the concept of boundaries has emerged as one of the most helpful contributions to the counseling community. You may already be familiar with this concept of setting external boundaries with others, such as maintaining healthy emotional distance and saying no when it's appropriate to do so. Have you considered, however, that just as you can set boundaries with other people, you can also set boundaries with overwhelming parts of yourself?

As members of the counseling community, we have benefited from the watershed book series by Henry Cloud and John Townsend, who have popularized the helpful concept of boundaries. Throughout this series, they acknowledge the *inner* work that accompanies setting healthy external boundaries with others. A chapter called "Resistance to Boundaries" in their original book gives some examples of internal boundary issues that are important to address, including "angry reactions," "guilt messages," "unresolved grief and loss," "fear of anger," and "fear of the unknown."[2]

I, Kim, was so interested in this idea of internal boundaries that I approached Townsend after hearing him speak at a conference. We had a brief exchange as he was dashing off to meet a client. "Walk and talk?" he quipped with a grin as I launched into my questions. Racing through the winding hallways, I asked, "What has most influenced your thinking about boundaries?" He stopped in his tracks and replied, "The Bible! The book *Boundaries* includes over three hundred scripture verses that relate to boundaries."

Indeed, the Bible has much to say about boundaries—not only in interpersonal relationships but also in the human soul. The apostle Paul described his own struggle with internal boundaries when he wrote, "I don't really understand myself, for I want to do what is right, but I don't do it. Instead, I do what I hate" (Rom. 7:15 NLT). That's to say, a part of Paul was crossing a boundary that another part of him wanted to keep. The book you hold in your hands focuses on the universal struggle of feeling internally divided. It shows you how to work with the conflicted aspects of yourself so you can improve your external relationships too.

Internal boundaries strengthen the connection between the sacred place inside your soul and various parts of yourself. For reasons explained in chapter 2, we call this process of creating healthy boundaries within your soul "Spirit-led self-leadership." Good internal boundaries empower you to live from the essential you, your soul in its purest and holiest state. From this place, you can faithfully lead your troubling thoughts and emotions. This work of building strong internal boundaries involves practicing the presence of God while being attuned to the parts of yourself that need your attention. It involves inviting God's Spirit into the farthest reaches of who you are.

BECOME A STUDENT OF THE MANY FACETS OF YOUR SOUL

At some point, you may have realized it's not just the problems and challenging people surrounding you that rob your life of joy. Like everyone, you have been wounded and have developed patterns that limit your ability to be your best self and experience lasting peace. Internal challenges, such as anger, guilt, and unforgiveness require your attention, or you end up overwhelmed and hurting others unnecessarily. It's hard to be good to others when you're hurting inside.

And ironically, the most natural way of addressing troubling emotions actually makes things worse. Many well-meaning people seek to suppress and even condemn aspects of themselves they don't like. The most common response to unwanted impulses is to insist, *I need to get over it* or, *I've got to stop thinking that way.* In our experience as counselors, we've found that this approach rarely works.

This book presents another way. A different means to the same end. A slower way to get where you want to go—faster. It's the "Come . . . let us reason together" approach (Isa. 1:18 KJV). It involves understanding and even befriending the hurting parts of your soul.

> **Mature love is extending hospitality—even toward the parts of your soul that are angry, fearful, anxious, or sad.**

This suggestion may seem counterintuitive. *Befriend my anger and fear?* you may be thinking. *That's the last thing I want to do.* Consider this: Jesus taught us to love our enemies. "Pray for those who persecute you," he said (Matt. 5:44). When you throw a dinner party, stretch yourself and invite the unpopular people (Luke 14:12–14). Mature love is extending hospitality—even toward the parts of your soul that are angry, fearful, anxious, or sad.

As you listen to them, you'll discover that these emotions represent distinct parts of your soul that need your care. You'll realize that some are too close to the essential you, and some are too far away. You'll get to know overbearing aspects of yourself you wish would give you some space, as well as disowned, denied, and lost facets of your personality hiding in the shadows. All of these parts of you, whether too near or too far, exist for a reason. They need for you to create healthy boundaries with them so you can relate to them from a comfortable distance. Your emotional well-being depends on it, as does the quality of your relationships.

Boundaries for Your Soul is the first book that focuses entirely on applying boundaries concepts to your internal thoughts and feelings. As we've studied this topic, the most useful resource for us has been the Internal Family Systems model (IFS).[3] This fast-growing, proven therapy model is helping many people discover internal harmony and wholeness.[4] This book presents an approach that integrates boundaries concepts with IFS concepts—interpreted through a Christian lens. We've developed this Christian approach to IFS because, ultimately, the best way to care for the overwhelming parts of your soul involves inviting God's Holy Spirit to be with them.

The best way to care for the overwhelming parts of your soul involves inviting God's Holy Spirit to be with them.

Through our counseling work and in our own lives, we've seen firsthand how powerful this approach is, and we believe it can change your life too. Here's what we know: When you think of your unwanted thoughts and feelings as belonging to parts of your soul, you begin to see how they relate to one another and to the core of your being, where the Holy Spirit abides. And just as you can experience a more peaceful life as a result of healthy boundaries with others, you can also establish helpful boundaries with the parts of your soul. Imagine these various parts as members of an internal family, and your Spirit-led self, like a good parent, leading these parts with courage and love.

THE WAY FORWARD

To get started, chapter 1 demonstrates how you can be out of touch with some parts of your soul and overwhelmed by others. The chapter ends with a lighthearted Internal Boundaries Quiz (p. 14) to help you pinpoint your strengths and growth opportunities. Next we discuss the Spirit-led self, capable of leading your thoughts and feelings. Then we explore more specifically the inevitable challenges that arise within your inner world. You'll get to know three categories of parts in your soul. And you'll become equipped to lead and care for them more effectively, because "understanding is the basis of care."[5] That's part I.

Part II presents a five-step process to help you bring together all you know of God with all you're experiencing right now. We show you how to *focus on, befriend, invite God to be with, unburden,* and *integrate* parts of your soul. You'll learn how to work with your overwhelming thoughts and feelings so you can enjoy peace within.

We've packed part III with additional guidance to help you apply the Five Steps to specific emotions that may be troubling you. You'll learn ways that the most conflicted parts of yourself, warring within, could become your greatest allies. Along the way, we'll explore questions such as:

- How can I be less critical and learn to control my anger?
- Is there anything I can do about my anxiety and fear?
- Will I always be weighed down with sadness?
- What do I do with my envy and desire?
- Is there any way to be free from guilt and shame?

As you grow in putting your thoughts and feelings to work for your highest good, you'll know what to do when you feel overwhelmed. You'll move from anger to advocacy, from shame to joy, and your inner critic will become your champion. It's a journey toward wholeness that will change you forever and lead to a life of joyful service to others. We're excited for you to experience the freedom that comes from building healthy boundaries in your soul.

Part I

REIMAGINING YOUR SOUL

A part of you was left behind very early in your life: the part that never felt completely received. It is full of fears. Meanwhile, you grew up with many survival skills. But you want yourself to be one.

—Henri Nouwen, *The Inner Voice of Love*

Chapter 1

WHY BOUNDARIES FOR YOUR SOUL?

I don't really understand myself, for I want to do what is right, but I don't do it. Instead, I do what I hate.

—THE APOSTLE PAUL (ROMANS 7:15 NLT)

MEGAN FACED BURNOUT. Hoping to restore her soul, she settled into a lovely retreat center with an ocean view. The peaceful backdrop was everything she hoped it would be. She soon discovered, however, that sitting quietly only made her more anxious. Unable to quell the competing thoughts in her mind, she gave up and started streaming her favorite show. Megan desired to rest, but her racing thoughts refused to slow down.

❧

"What's wrong with me?" Ruben moaned, slouched in his counselor's office chair. "I'm tired of falling asleep alone on the couch every night." Ruben had no difficulty attracting women, but he didn't trust himself to play the dating game without getting into trouble. In fact, he was in a double bind: he longed for a meaningful relationship, yet he wanted to avoid the confusing emotions that came from being close to another person. Not knowing what to do with these conflicting desires, he worried he would never experience lasting love.

⊛

"To be honest, I wish I had my best friend's life," Jenna said over coffee. "Yesterday, I caught myself daydreaming about an enormous wave dousing her family during their beachside Christmas-card photo shoot. It bothers me that her life seems so perfect while mine is such a struggle. I ask God to take my jealousy away, but my prayers never seem to help. Honestly, I'm beginning to think that whoever's up there has given up on me." On one hand, Jenna wanted to care about people, but on the other hand, she wrestled with her unfulfilled longings. Jenna didn't know what to do with her envy or the nagging guilt that inevitably ensued.

⊛

Tom couldn't face the thought of telling his wife that he had been denied the promotion and raise they had counted on all year. He worked hard to suppress the feeling of shame about not providing more for his family. Being passed over triggered the familiar refrain: *I'm such a loser—I'll never amount to anything.* Tom's sense of shame was preventing him from sharing his feelings with his wife. "Great day!" he feigned, greeting her the evening he received the disappointing news. It wasn't hard to predict that Tom soon would be ambushed by a mob of unruly emotions.

⊛

"A part of me hates being the bad guy, but another part of me gets so annoyed with incompetence!" exclaimed Lin, a pediatric resident,

4

pounding the table with her fist. "My colleagues at the hospital always slow me down." Her supervisors' evaluations were unanimous: *Excellent clinical skills. . . . Doesn't work well with others. . . . Serious attitude problem.* In response to this feedback, Lin knew she should hold her tongue. But regardless of how much she tried to restrain herself, her volcanic rage still managed to erupt. No one would expect such a competent professional to feel so out of control.

WHAT'S THE PROBLEM?

Megan, Ruben, Jenna, Tom, and Lin don't know what to do with the difficult thoughts and feelings ruling their lives, so they feel overwhelmed and behave in ways they regret. Each of them is caught in a minefield of shoulds, can'ts, and what-were-you-thinkings. The more they try to forge ahead, the worse they feel.

Can you identify in some way with their inner turmoil? You work hard, try to set boundaries with others, and then wonder why you still struggle with anger, fear, and guilt. You may even hurt the people you love the most as a result of these unwanted feelings—petty jealousies you can't rein in, fear-based workaholism, or an out-of-control temper that you know isn't you.

When you're strong inside, you're able to respond with more resilience to life's challenges. You'll be true to the person God created you to be and to the work he has planned for you to do. You'll be realistic about your limitations and have a clear sense of your own values, vision, mission, and priorities. You'll understand that the health of your relationships and the sustainability of your service depend on your ability to make wise decisions about how you spend your time.

That's where this book can help. We'll walk you through a process of establishing healthy boundaries with the various parts of your soul that are competing for control. And you'll discover that the better you become at establishing internal boundaries, the better you'll become at setting healthy boundaries with others too.

soul
/sōl/
noun
"the . . . feeling, thought, and action in humans, regarded as a distinct entity separate from the body"[1]

Caring for your soul, with its many thoughts and feelings, involves understanding more about it. Respected philosopher of religion Dallas Willard wrote that the soul includes all of the nonphysical dimensions of a person. In this book, when we speak of the soul, we simply mean the nonphysical part of who you are.

Dallas Willard also explains that the soul "can be significantly 'reprogrammed' and this . . . is a major part of what goes into the spiritual formation (re-formation) of the person."[2] In other words, when you care for your soul, you are reprogramming—or reforming—the contours of your internal life. You are reshaping and redefining your thoughts and feelings and inevitably your actions too. And you are taking responsibility for creating and maintaining strong internal boundaries.

TOO CLOSE OR TOO FAR?

boundary
/boun-dree/ or /bound(ə)rē/
noun
"something that indicates bounds or limits; a limiting or bounding line"[3]

What are boundaries? Your "boundaries" are the borders or limits of who you are and what you do, and what behaviors (your own and those of others) you will and will not accept. Your spirit, mind, heart, will, and body all have boundaries. Understanding these limits helps you honor your individuality and the individuality of others.

To use an external boundary as an example, when you have a conversation with another person, you don't stand so close that you step on her toes or so far away that you yell from a distance. Instead, you stand at arm's reach so that the two of you can hear each other comfortably. As another example, if a good friend moves away, you may feel too far from him and need to find new ways to maintain your connection. On the other hand, if he were to crowd you emotionally, you would need to get some space. You may feel too far from an estranged relative whom you haven't seen in years or too close to an overbearing one who visits too often and stays too long. Essentially, you can draw closer to people at will or move farther away in order to establish *comfortable distance*.

Likewise, there are two opposite, unhealthy ways of relating to your painful emotions. You can keep them too close to you, or you can push them too far away. If they're too close, you risk being overwhelmed by them. If they're too far, you risk being cut off from them, only to be influenced by them in harmful ways.

You may wonder why you would ever want to draw painful feelings in closer. *Isn't it better to keep them away?* Think of it this way: Your painful emotions are being experienced by parts of your soul that need to be heard, honored, and understood in order for you to be able to help them. Furthermore, the parts of your soul experiencing these difficult emotions have much to teach you when you get to know them. As with the people in your life, the key is to establish comfortable distance with these parts of your soul.

7

So, how do you know when painful emotions are too close or too far?

When you're *too close to* painful emotions, you might have thoughts like these:

> *Other people always let me down.* (victimization)
> *I'll keep giving and suffering for everyone else's sake.*
>   (martyrdom)
> *It's always going to be this way . . . I'll never be happy.*
>   (hopelessness)

When you are *too far from* painful emotions, you might find yourself thinking things like this:

> *She made me get angry. She's the problem!* (blaming)
> *It's too painful to talk about . . . I'll just change the subject.*
>   (avoiding)
> *What hopes and dreams? Dreaming hurts too much. My life is fine
>   the way it is.* (denying)

If you're experiencing victimization, martyrdom, or hopelessness, you might be too close to painful feelings and stuck in a rut of old habits and beliefs. This way of life robs you of confidence and joy. On the other hand, if you tend toward blaming, avoiding, and denying, you're trying to keep your painful feelings far away. You're disowning important gifts that the parts of you experiencing these feelings have to offer. What's more, denied emotions don't actually go away. Instead, they reappear in even more harmful ways. It's like playing a game of whack-a-mole at the fair. You hit one pesky emotion down with a mallet, only to have it pop up again when you least expect it. To lead emotions effectively, you can focus on them, befriend them, and invite Jesus to be near—then unburden them and integrate them

with the other parts of your soul. We call this process taking a
You-Turn.

TAKING A YOU-TURN

Most clients come to us initially with the desire to talk about *someone else*—their spouse, boss, child, friend, and so on. We get it:
when conflict detonates a frenzy of emotion, the natural response
is to become reactive and to accuse *the other*. Jesus addressed this
tendency to blame others. In his Sermon on the Mount, he challenged the crowd to work on their own personal growth: "First
take the plank out of your own eye, and then you will see clearly to
remove the speck from your brother's eye" (Matt. 7:5).

Jesus wants you to get to know the state of your soul. When
you're feeling angry, what else is going on inside of you? Is there
another part of you that's hurting? If so, it needs to be drawn in
closer so you can give it the care it needs. Or, is there a part of
you that has become reckless and needs some
gentle boundaries? Notice the cues. Listen to
your pain. When conflicted emotions threaten
to derail you, seize the opportunity to evalu-
ate your internal boundaries. What thoughts

**Internal conflict is
growth trying to
happen.**

and feelings need your time, attention, and redirection? These
overwhelming parts of your soul present opportunities for your
growth and healing. After all, internal conflict is growth trying
to happen.[4]

But wait! That person said such cruel things! a part of you might be
piping up. And that may be true. Whether or not you were provoked
unjustly, however, it's most helpful to notice how *you* responded to
the situation. Taking a You-Turn helps you gain clarity about your
own thoughts and feelings so you can respond intentionally instead
of becoming overwhelmed.

So, to take a You-Turn, follow these Five Steps:

Step 1: **Focus** on an overwhelming part of yourself.
Step 2: **Befriend** this part you don't like.
Step 3: **Invite** Jesus to draw near.
Step 4: **Unburden** this weary part.
Step 5: **Integrate** it into your internal team of rivals.[5]

We'll explore this approach in the pages ahead. As you engage in this process, you'll move from seeing your undesirable inclinations as problems to seeing them as allies on your path to peace and wholeness. You'll become more curious about your troubling thoughts and emotions instead of disliking them. This compassionate posture toward yourself will help you develop what have been called "those wise restraints that make [us] free."[6]

AN ANCIENT STRUGGLE

History has much to teach us about the importance of taking a You-Turn. People have been blaming others instead of taking responsibility for their feelings since the dawn of time. We can learn from their mistakes.

Consider Adam and Eve. Eve was overwhelmed by desire when the serpent tempted her to eat the fruit that God had told them not to eat. She gave in to a part of herself that took what was not hers to have. Adam, meanwhile, avoided his guilty feelings. When God asked if he had eaten the forbidden fruit, he said, in essence, "Don't look at me!" What if Eve had paused for a moment when she felt her longing—and obeyed God? And what if Adam had acknowledged his guilt instead of blaming Eve?

Consider Sarah, the wife of the biblical patriarch Abraham. God promised Abraham that Sarah would birth a great nation, but Sarah thought she was too old to conceive. Afraid to face her own limitations, she yielded to an impulse to take control and get what she wanted in her own way. She arranged for her maidservant, Hagar, to sleep with her husband and bear his child. Then, in a fit of envy, she banished Hagar to the desert (Gen. 16:1–4; 21:8–14). Overwhelmed by fear, Sarah created a complicated love triangle and even attempted murder. What if, instead, Sarah had let Abraham know that she was afraid she wouldn't be able to live up to others' expectations? (Sarah later shows up in the Bible's "Hall of Faith" chapter, Hebrews 11, so we know she somehow found her way.)

Or what about Peter? Peter vowed his commitment to Jesus many times, including when it made him unpopular. But even loyal Peter let his fear of being identified with a revolutionary outlaw overwhelm him when crowd members began to accuse him. He denied he knew Jesus three times, betraying the One who most loved him and whom he had left his way of life to follow (Mark 14:66–72). Like Sarah, Peter eventually faced his shame, developed a humble heart, and fulfilled his calling, becoming the person Jesus called the "rock" of the church (Matt. 16:18).

Lastly, let's look again at King David. As discussed in the introduction, a war was waging within his soul. One evening his wandering eye caught a beautiful woman bathing in the moonlight. Yielding to his longing to possess her, David slept with Bathsheba, even though she was married. Then, succumbing to a conniving part that wanted to hide what he had done, he arranged to have her husband killed. David let desire run roughshod over his truest self, and he ended up committing murder (2 Sam. 11).

The prophet Nathan eventually helped David come to his senses by telling him a story about a rich man who stole a poor man's one and only sheep. "He must pay!" David exclaimed, burning with anger. Then Nathan revealed, "You are the man!" (2 Sam. 12:1–7). King David ultimately faced his internal conflict and restored fellowship with God. As he matured, he composed a song conveying how he had learned to set boundaries with his unruly emotions: "I have calmed and quieted my soul," he wrote, "like a . . . child within me" (Ps. 131:2 AMP).

THE POWER OF COMPASSION

What do these well-known Bible characters and the everyday people at the beginning of this chapter have in common? All were, at one point, overwhelmed by strong emotions. They all have warring factions in their souls.

Though the Bible stories above may seem extreme, in many ways they reveal the kind of inner conflicts we all experience. *I think I'm a good person,* and yet, like the apostle Paul, you realize, "I do not do what I want, but I do the very thing I hate" (Rom. 7:15 ESV). Likewise, the apostle James described people as at times being "double-minded" (James 1:8). A person can pray one minute and say a hurtful word the next. "Out of the same mouth come praise and cursing" (3:10).

Have you ever said, "I want to be kind, but I'm so angry"? Or "I know I should move on, but I can't stop thinking about him"? If you find it hard to resolve painful feelings and unhelpful thoughts, you're not alone. Everyone feels overwhelmed at times by conflicting feelings. You want to live a good life, to be a loving person, but sometimes you hurt others and even yourself.

Is there anything that can be done? As Christian counselors, we have discovered—*yes,* there is. You can relate in a compassionate way with these aspects of yourself in need of attention. You can hone your capacity to listen to your sometimes-chaotic inner world and prayerfully lead the parts of your soul in working for your highest good.

Imagine if Megan, on a retreat to escape burnout, gained perspective and learned to pay attention to her racing thoughts. Might she be able to connect with God in an empowering way? If Ruben reconciled his conflicting desires, might he find true love? If Jenna listened to her envy, might she gain insight into qualities that she herself was longing to develop? If Tom gained perspective about his shame, might he be able to share his sorrow with

Every part of you has tremendous potential for good.

his wife and, in doing so, experience the joy of true intimacy? And if Lin grew to understand her anger, might she be able to care for her subtle but deep fear of rejection and advocate effectively for herself?

In the pages that follow, you'll learn how to achieve the life-changing results of taking a You-Turn—a process of caring for your soul. We'll present a proven way to help you move from reacting to or avoiding difficult situations, to acting intentionally.[7] As a result, you'll become gentler with yourself and speak more constructively with others about how you're doing. You'll enjoy greater peace within and experience deeper intimacy with others too.

If you lead painful emotions with perspective, guided by the Holy Spirit, you'll discover that every part of you has tremendous potential for good. You'll live at a comfortable distance from the challenging aspects of your soul, relating to each one in a caring way. You'll learn when to say yes and how to say no to your thoughts and feelings.[8] You can bring together what you know of God with what you're experiencing in any given moment and enjoy the benefits of boundaries for your soul.

Before you move on to the next chapter, we invite you to take our lighthearted quiz to gain insight into the current state of your internal boundaries.

INTERNAL BOUNDARIES QUIZ
Are your emotions too close or too far?

In each of the following scenarios, choose the answer closest to how you would respond:

1. You're tired of seeing Facebook pictures of your neighbor's successful spouse, charming children, and delightful dinner parties, so you:
   a. post your best photos, including one of your dog jumping through a flaming hula hoop, and enroll your entire family in a ninety-day self-improvement boot camp.
   b. gush to your neighbor about her photos and thank her for being such a blessing in your life.
   c. feel guilty about being envious and relieved that others can't read your mind.
   d. notice your envy and take a break from social media.

2. Before you were hired, your manager promised that weekend work wouldn't be necessary, but today marks the fifth straight weekend he's enlisted your help at the office. You:
   a. decline and spend the weekend feeling guilty.
   b. show up to work but quietly stew as you think of your friends having fun without you.
   c. process with a friend why you're afraid to tell your boss how you feel.
   d. agree to work and then drown your sorrows with a pint of Ben & Jerry's Chunky Monkey.

3. Over lunch with friends, a member of your small group tearfully shares that last night her husband yelled at her and then spent the night on the couch. You:
   a. politely excuse yourself. Public angsting makes you queasy.

14

    b. tell her what a jerk he is and say you'll pray for her.

    c. share your sadness about what happened and notice what else you're feeling.

    d. chime in with your own stories of marriage woes.

4. Your mother-in-law stops by for a visit. After leaving the kitchen momentarily, you return to find her rearranging the art on the wall—again. You:

    a. bite your tongue and complain later to your spouse.

    b. notice your anger, consider its origin, and come up with a plan for how to address future boundary crossings.

    c. covet your friend's mother-in-law who helpfully babysits.

    d. say you love the rearranged art while she's still in your home, but then return it to its original location after she leaves.

5. You were passed over for a promotion you had been working hard to obtain. You:

    a. tell yourself to get over it, even though you don't know how to do that.

    b. feel sorry for yourself and wonder why things never go your way.

    c. pray with a friend about your disappointment.

    d. daydream about ways to undermine your new boss.

6. You've spent too much money eating out recently, and you're having trouble paying off your credit card debt. You aren't sure whether to tell your significant other. You:

    a. decide to face the painful feelings you've been avoiding by going on so many spending sprees.

    b. don't bring up the issue. If he or she doesn't ask, why should you tell?

    c. hyperventilate at the mere thought of your credit card bill.

    d. become depressed about your dwindling bank account.

7. It's day two of a weeklong vacation, and you're struggling. Yesterday you completed your to-do list of relaxation activities. Today you can't stop thinking about work. You:
   a. call the office to check in. The team said everything will be fine in your absence, but you'll feel better if you check.
   b. ponder why you feel anxious whenever you're away from work.
   c. stay in bed with the shutters closed and fret about all you're not getting done.
   d. refrain from calling the office, but thoroughly detail your rental car.

8. You're running late to meet friends for lunch when your significant other stops the car at a yellow light. You:
   a. say, "Way to save money, babe! At this rate, we can skip lunch and arrive just in time for dinner."
   b. educate your significant other that yellow means "Speed up!"
   c. kindly share that you're feeling anxious.
   d. sigh loudly, hoping to be asked what's wrong.

9. Whether you would rather take your—lately very unruly—kids with you to the grocery store or drink from your dog's water bowl is a toss-up. Even so, the inevitable day has arrived. You:
   a. stare enviously at others' well-behaved kids quietly walking beside their parents' carts.
   b. resolve to be gentle with yourself even if you lose your cool.
   c. mutter, "Who's been raising these kids, anyway?" as the canned goods display topples.
   d. decide to bypass the mania altogether this month. McDonald's isn't looking so bad after all.

10. Your big presentation is tomorrow, but it's 10 p.m. and you're still stuck on the first slide. You:
    a. rework the color scheme again, hoping your seventh attempt results in perfection.

b. condemn yourself for not starting the project until now.
c. resolve to call in sick tomorrow, then spend the next four hours catching up on your favorite TV series.
d. decide your presentation doesn't have to be perfect—good enough will do.

INTERNAL BOUNDARIES QUIZ SCORING AND RESULTS

Scoring:
Give yourself 1 point for each of the following answers:
1d, 2c, 3c, 4b, 5c, 6a, 7b, 8c, 9b, 10d
Give yourself 0 points for any other answer.

YOUR TOTAL SCORE IS: _____

If your total score is 0–3:
You're too far from your emotions, and this book can help!

Based on your answers, you tend to avoid painful feelings. You might feel like a victim of your circumstances. You have difficulty speaking up on behalf of yourself, and you often bury what you feel and think. This book will teach you to face your emotions and turn them into powerful allies.

If your total score is 4–7:
Some of your emotions are too close, some are too far, and some are at a comfortable distance. Learn which emotions are troubling you, and put them to work for you!

Although you work hard to manage your challenging emotions, sometimes you don't know what to do with them and end up increasing your anger, fear, anxiety, sadness, envy, guilt, or shame.

Chapter 9 addresses *anger*. Anger becomes a powerful ally when you learn to befriend it. We invite you to join us in discovering the benefits—and dangers—of your anger and how to care for

BOUNDARIES FOR YOUR SOUL

its unique needs. Can you imagine turning your critic into a trusted adviser?

Chapter 10 addresses *fear and anxiety*. It takes fear to have courage. You can listen to your anxiety and put it to work for you. You'll discover that when understood, these powerful feelings can point the way to God's still voice within.

Chapter 11 addresses *sadness*. You need your pain to help you grow and develop strong spiritual roots, but you don't need to let pain overwhelm you. When you welcome your sadness, it's more willing to work with you. You can set a gentle boundary with it so that it settles peacefully into one chamber of your heart.

Chapter 12 addresses *envy*. Can you imagine turning envy into your ally? Envy is a powerful emotion in response to parts of you that might feel left out or just plain stuck. Discover how you can listen to your envy and put it to work to motivate you in healthy ways.

Chapter 13 addresses *guilt and shame*. Is your inner critic ready to let go of the lies it has been believing? Are you ready to release a burden of shame? It's time to rewrite your narrative with courageous authenticity, in light of the bigger, better story that says, *You are loved.*

If your total score is 8–10:
You have healthy boundaries with your thoughts and feelings—they're at a comfortable distance! This book will provide you with ideas that you can use to help others.

You're aware of the importance of treating yourself with care and respect. You're adept at leading yourself faithfully in partnership with God. The content in this book will help you continue to turn your overwhelming thoughts and feelings into your greatest allies. Take a look at chapter 14 for ideas about how to be patient with the challenging parts of others and discover even greater intimacy with those you love.

18

Chapter 2

YOUR SPIRIT-LED SELF

I will give you a new heart and put a new spirit in you.
—Ezekiel 36:26

We have received . . . the Spirit who is from God.
—1 Corinthians 2:12

WHY DO WE all struggle with troubling thoughts and over-whelming emotions? Think of it this way: Your thoughts and feelings belong to distinct parts of your personality, and they're vying for control. Each of these well-meaning parts has its own agenda—its own ideas about how to think, feel, and act in any given moment. Each one contends for your attention and believes its strategy to be best. Megan's story provides a helpful example.

MEGAN FROM THE INSIDE OUT

Megan would have talked the whole session if I, Kim, hadn't cut in. The successful director of a respected organization, Megan was struggling in her marriage. She hated to admit that she wasn't speaking to the man sleeping on the far side of her bed.

When Megan was little, her family was the poorest on the block. At an early age, she committed to work hard and make plenty of money when she grew up. She dreamed of climbing the corporate ladder in addition to having a family. Now an adult, and by all external measures having achieved her goals, Megan still struggled with the fear of not having what her family needed to survive. And the only thing she knew to do was to work even harder.

In an early session, Megan explained that she wanted to feel close to her husband. When he would start sharing about his day, though, she would be overwhelmed by all she needed to get done. Despite her genuine desire to be a loving wife, a hardworking part of her that focused on tasks more than on people would take over. Instead of relaxing at home after work, she couldn't stop riffling through her mental to-do list. Time after dinner had devolved into a dash to get the dishes done, followed by a marathon meet-up with her emails and spreadsheets. This striving part of Megan was married to her work. As a result, it had been a year since she had enjoyed a conversation with her husband.

Megan's task manager reminded me of a character named Joy from one of my favorite movies. I suggested that Megan see *Inside Out* before our next session. "I'm curious whether you'll see any parallels between the movie and your life," I commented.

"Isn't that a kids' movie?" Megan asked, cautiously, eyeing the colorful plastic *Inside Out* figurines perched on my otherwise dignified bookshelves.

The movie explores what goes on in the inner world of a girl named Riley whose life is disrupted when her parents relocate the family from the Midwest to California. Each of Riley's emotions—her Anger, Fear, Sadness, Disgust, and Joy, also characters with the same names—competes to push its own agenda. I knew the example of Riley would help Megan grasp the nature of her own struggle and how her task manager was vying for control.

As the movie unfolds, Anger prompts Riley to lash out at her parents. Fear preempts Riley's efforts to make friends at her new school. Joy works overtime to keep Sadness from taking over the "headquarters" of her mind. All the while, her dad's Anger tries (and fails miserably) to bridle Riley's emotions, while her mom fantasizes about an imaginary muscular Brazilian helicopter pilot!

Sure enough, after watching the film, Megan ended up discovering many other parts of herself that were waiting to be seen and heard. How about you? Do you ever find yourself thinking, *A part of me feels sad, but another part feels angry*? Perhaps, like Megan, you might be taken over temporarily by a striving task manager, even though deep down you would prefer to connect with friends and loved ones. Or, like Riley, you may bowl people over with enthusiasm, even when another part of you is feeling lonely.

You don't have to be overwhelmed by your thoughts and feelings—you have the ability to lead them, guided by the Spirit of God.

The well-meaning, but quarreling, parts of your personality require healthy boundaries. Thankfully, you have what it takes to establish these boundaries and bring peace to the conflict within. You don't have to be overwhelmed by your thoughts and feelings—you have the ability to lead them, guided by the Spirit of God.

PARTICIPATING WITH GOD'S SPIRIT

Why are we convinced you have what it takes to shape and form your soul? Didn't the prophet Jeremiah warn, "The human heart is the most deceitful of all things, and desperately wicked" (Jer. 17:9 NLT)? Isn't he saying we shouldn't trust ourselves? Yes, but the same prophet who declared this bad news about our deceitful state also foretold the good news about what would happen one day when Jesus of Nazareth would come, live, die, and rise again.

Jeremiah conveyed the purpose of these revolutionary events with these words: "I will put my law in their minds and write it on their hearts" (Jer. 31:33).

Let's back up for a minute. Initially, God gave Moses the Ten Commandments—a written, external code—as a way to communicate his laws. These laws are wise standards that still apply today: don't worship false gods . . . don't create idols . . . don't take God's name in vain . . . take a weekly rest . . . honor your parents . . . don't murder . . . don't cheat . . . don't steal . . . don't lie . . . don't pine after others' possessions (Ex. 20:1–17). The problem was that the knowledge of these standards didn't empower God's people to live by them.

The truth is, no one lives up to the standards God gave Moses. We all violate these commands when we, for example: act selfishly; create idols of money, family, and popularity; bend the truth to get out of a mess we've made; harbor envy and animosity toward others; dishonor our families; and hurt our friends. We constantly mess up, and that's why Jeremiah lamented the terrible state of the human heart.

So God set in motion phase two of his plan: writing his law on the hearts of his followers. This second phase began with the birth of Jesus—who abided completely by God's laws, showing us how to live well. Jesus then gave up his life to pay the price for our inability to live perfectly. And as he prepared to die, he told his followers his Spirit would be with them: "I will ask the Father," he said, "and he will give you another Helper, to be with you forever, even the Spirit of truth. . . . You know him, for he dwells with you and will be in you" (John 14:16–17 ESV). Jesus showed us how to live, and now, in fulfillment of his promise, foretold by Jeremiah, he sends his Spirit to dwell in the hearts of all who would receive him.

God responds to human brokenness by transforming our souls from the inside out. To help us understand that his Spirit empowers us to live out the law, the resurrected Jesus first poured out his Spirit upon his disciples at Pentecost, the Jewish commemoration of the day God gave the Ten Commandments to the nation of Israel assembled at Mount Sinai. Centuries earlier Moses had received heavy stone tablets, but when the disciples gathered in the Upper Room, as recorded in Acts 2, God wrote his law *on their hearts.*

Today, we have the law as a written code; we have Jesus' example and teaching; and if you have welcomed Jesus into your heart, you have his Spirit living inside of you as the ultimate source of wisdom and healing power. The focus of this book is to help you access the Spirit of God abiding in your soul and to encourage you to invite his Spirit to be near those parts of your soul needing his care.

Having the Holy Spirit within doesn't automatically bring perfect peace and joy, however, because some parts of your soul can be stubborn and resist God's will. In any moment, you can choose whether to walk with the Spirit or to go your own way.

Thankfully, you can play an active role in connecting the troubled parts of yourself to the Holy Spirit who dwells inside of you. You can invite him to be with them, and you can witness his power at work—in partnership with God you can befriend and lead the unruly parts of your soul into an abundant life (John 10:10). Jesus said, "I am the vine; you are the branches.

In any moment, you can choose whether to walk with the Spirit or to go your own way.

If you remain in me and I in you, you will bear much fruit" (John 15:5). All parts of you can abide in Christ, as he abides in you.

God has given you agency. He invites you to participate in the work he is doing in your life. Your task is to trust neither your thoughts nor your feelings, but to *lead* them in step with God's Spirit. As you do, you can turn the most challenging parts of your soul into your greatest allies.

Human Initiative and Divine Blessing

The Bible's story of Ruth teaches that divine blessing can work hand in hand with human initiative. At the beginning of the story, we learn that Ruth's husband has died. Ruth's mother-in-law, Naomi, asks God for a new husband for her widowed daughter-in-law. In addition to praying, Naomi takes initiative. She suggests that Ruth pick grain alongside the workers of a respected man named Boaz. In the end, God provides: Ruth and Boaz are married, and Naomi praises God for his faithfulness. This biblical story, and many others, conveys the idea that God often uses human initiative to fulfill his plans.

WELCOME TO YOUR SPIRIT-LED SELF

When you open your heart to the Holy Spirit, you receive a living treasure who assists with this process of guiding and restoring the fragmented facets of your soul (2 Cor. 4:7 ESV). The apostle Paul wrote to the Ephesians, "When you believed, you were marked in him with a seal, the promised Holy Spirit" (Eph. 1:13). As a result, he strengthens you "with power through his Spirit in your inner being, so that Christ may dwell in your hearts through faith . . . that you may be filled with all the fullness of God" (3:16–17, 19 ESV). And in another letter Paul wrote, "For I delight in the law of God, in my inner being" (Rom. 7:22 ESV). These words *inner being* describe who you are at your core: your Holy Spirit–led self—or what we call your "Spirit-led self" for short.

Your Creator has imbued your body and soul with a remarkable ability to heal themselves to a certain extent. And though your soul can heal somewhat without external intervention, your journey toward wholeness is far more powerful when you have the Spirit inside. As a doctor would care for an injured part of your body, so you can care for troubled parts of your soul with the help of God's Spirit.

Your Spirit-led self is you when you are being led by God, who abides within your soul. Many psychologists and spiritual leaders have explored this idea of what we're calling the Spirit-led self. For example, beloved author Henri Nouwen described that place in your soul where you have clear perspective, where you can gather together your thoughts and desires and hold them together in truth.

Nouwen, a Holland-born priest and professor, wrote about this sacred place while in the throes of a personal emotional struggle. Seeking wholeness, he spent eleven years living and serving in L'Arche, a community for people with disabilities. Nouwen's personal journaling during these years formed the basis for his profound work *The Inner Voice of Love*. This insightful book demonstrates how Nouwen, guided by God's Spirit within, befriended his feelings of fear, sadness, guilt, and shame, inviting Jesus to minister to his painful emotions. He wrote:

> You have to trust that there is another place . . . where you can be safe. Maybe it is wrong to think about this new place as beyond emotions, passions, and feelings. *Beyond* could suggest that these human sentiments are absent there. Instead, try thinking about this place as the core of your being—your heart, where all human sentiments are held together in truth. From this place you can feel, think, and act truthfully.[1]

Likewise, psychologists Henry Cloud and John Townsend refer to a "space inside" where you can experience your feelings without fear of judgment—a place where these parts of your soul can receive the attention they need so you don't act in hurtful ways:

"We need to have spaces inside ourselves where we can have a feeling, an impulse, or a desire, without acting it out," they wrote. "We need self-control without repression."[2]

In this place, your Spirit-led self "holds you together in truth." From here you can draw a troubling emotion in closer or ask it to step back, so you can develop perspective. You can invite Jesus to be with the parts of you most in need of his presence. Your Spirit-led self can minister to your troubling thoughts and feelings, so that they are witnessed and transformed.

You know that you're leading from your Spirit-led self when you're experiencing any of the following qualities, all of which begin with the letter c:[3]

- calmness
- clarity
- curiosity
- compassion
- confidence
- courage
- creativity
- connectedness

You're also leading from the Spirit-led self when you are manifesting any of the fruit of the Spirit: love, joy, peace, patience, kindness, goodness, faithfulness, gentleness, and self-control (Gal. 5:22–23 ESV).

As you embark on this journey through the pages ahead, take this understanding of the Spirit-led self with you. It can be difficult to face your thoughts and feelings. But attuning to the challenging, painful, sometimes dark aspects of your soul creates a connection with them that God can use to strengthen you from within, and "you'll be changed from the inside out" (Rom. 12:1–2 MSG). Guided by the Holy Spirit, you can weather the storms of life with hope.

SPIRIT-LED SELF-LEADERSHIP

We call this process of guiding various parts of your soul *Spirit-led self-leadership*.[4] It involves taking charge of your soul with courage and compassion. It means keeping your eyes on the road and your hands on the wheel.

Imagine you're a school bus driver, but instead of driving, you're sitting in the back row, hoping for the best. Little kids take turns at the steering wheel as the bus jolts this way and that. The kids are scared, but they don't know what else to do except wrestle for the wheel. Finally, you stand up, walk forward calmly, and take charge. The kids settle down, relieved that a capable adult is finally taking the lead.

Like in a runaway bus, problems arise in your soul when various parts of you wrestle for the wheel. In fact, you can think of any emotional issue as a cluster of entrenched parts that have taken over the leadership of the soul. You're not living with calm, clear leadership. You lose your sense of perspective. Chaos ensues, and you feel completely overwhelmed. Change starts with realizing, *I'm letting the kids drive the bus!* You have what it takes to take charge of your unruly thoughts and feelings when you're leading from your Spirit-led self.

♀
You Are Here

Here's the big picture so far:

- Your soul is composed of many parts, and some of these parts cause you strife.

- You also have within your soul a Spirit-led self, the wise grown-up inside, so to speak, full of wisdom and compassion.
- From this place, you can establish comfortable distance with all parts of yourself and lead them to become your greatest allies.

This work of building healthy boundaries within involves prayerfully inviting God to be with the parts of yourself that need your care. It means connecting with the hurting parts of your soul, befriending them, and leading them from your Spirit-led self.

CALLING ALL THEOLOGY INSPECTORS

You might have an internal theology inspector who's thinking, *What? You want me to befriend the troublesome parts of my soul? What if those parts of me are being influenced by powers of darkness in the spiritual realm?*

That's a good question. Good parents are careful about whom they let their children befriend, because dangerous people can destroy lives. You don't want to befriend the spiritual enemy of your soul who "prowls around like a roaring lion looking for someone to devour" (1 Peter 5:8). Sometimes the enemy may be influencing you. Or at times you may be overwhelmed by a part of yourself that simply needs befriending.[5]

You might be concerned that we're suggesting you befriend your sin, but that is not so. Instead, we encourage you to embrace the *part* of you that's sinning and that needs help changing, much as you would help a young child learn right from wrong. A good parent wouldn't shame or berate a child but first would connect with the child in a loving way. Only after making that connection would the parent begin to address the child's behavior. In a similar way, you can turn away from your sinful patterns without rejecting the parts of your soul that need your help to change.

Embrace a part but not its sin—befriend the former and turn away from the latter. God created Adam and Eve in his likeness and called them "good" (Gen. 1:31). You're called to accept yourself because you are made in God's image. When parts of yourself overwhelm you with destructive inclinations, however, you must lead from your Spirit-led self and establish strong internal boundaries.

When it comes to sin, it's not wise to condone the parts of your soul with thoughts, feelings, and behaviors that *miss the mark* (the meaning of the Greek word from which we get the verb *to sin*). On the other hand, it's not helpful to criticize yourself. The path to freedom involves clarifying sin before God. Clarifying what is sin does not require shaming and condemning; you can do so in a way that is loving, kind, and leads to repentance and abundant life.

What if each morning or night you were to kneel before God and give expression to the parts of yourself not yet abiding with him? You might envision the parts that carry your pride, your anger, and your shame sitting around a table or in a circle in front of you. As you lift them up, offer a prayer of confession on their behalf. And as they wait expectantly, let each one be seen and loved by the Savior.

OUR PROMISE TO YOU

As you better understand your soul and the parts of yourself that have overwhelmed you, you might discover you have a lot to learn. By focusing on them, you might become aware of important experiences from your past that continue to influence some of your behaviors today. Or you may become aware of extreme beliefs certain parts carry, even though you know in your heart that these beliefs aren't true.

By God's grace, your Spirit-led self has everything you need to care for hurting aspects of your soul—whether too close or too far—and to create strong internal boundaries. "He has given you everything you need for life and godliness" (2 Peter 1:3, paraphrased). When your Spirit-led self is leading, troubling parts of yourself gain perspective, let go of their extreme beliefs, and take on helpful roles. Can you imagine the sense of accomplishment from asking an angry or hurting part of yourself to give you a bit more space—and having it cooperate? Establishing healthy boundaries with your emotions is possible. We've seen it work, and we're confident you can do it.

As you embark on this journey, here's what we know: *Boundaries for Your Soul* provides a way for you to bring together what you know of God with the emotions you're experiencing right now so that you can have lasting joy.

Let's now explore three types of parts in your soul, because in the wise words of philosopher Dallas Willard, "understanding is the basis of care."[6]

Chapter 3

THREE PARTS OF YOU

Every major school of psychology has acknowledged
the mosaic nature of the human soul.
—Bessel van der Kolk

Give me an undivided heart, that I may fear your name.
—Psalm 86:11

"There's no one right framework for the soul," said Christian psychiatrist and author of *Anatomy of the Soul*, Curt Thompson. "What's important is that you *have* a framework and that it makes you more like Jesus."[1] We've found one that does just that. This model was developed in the 1990s, when psychologist Richard C. Schwartz noticed that people tend to talk about themselves in terms of "parts." And they describe these parts as having distinct thoughts, feelings, and character traits, like individual members of a family. Each part also carries its own story—a narrative about its role in the person's inner world. Based on these observations, he developed a theory called the Internal Family Systems model, or IFS. This evidence-based model provides a helpful way of categorizing the distinctive parts within the human soul and suggests a step-by-step approach to leading them into their most valuable states.[2]

This book presents an approach that integrates concepts from this IFS model with popular boundaries principles viewed through a Christian lens, because we believe that ultimately the best way to care for the troubled parts of your soul is to invite the Holy Spirit to lead them. This holistic framework introduces a way to care for your thoughts, feelings, and behaviors. It's biblical, simple, and—best of all—it works.

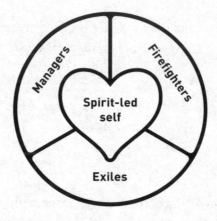

MAP OF THE SOUL

Just as you're created with specific physical traits (eye color and height, for example), you're also created with different parts of your soul. These parts develop over time. When they're hurt, rejected, or traumatized, they can take on extreme thoughts and feelings, and painful memories can weigh them down. And then they can cause you to behave in ways you wish you wouldn't. The goal, however, is not to get rid of your soul's parts—which would be impossible anyway—but to help them heal, grow, and discover their valuable, God-given roles.[3]

Schwartz identified three categories of parts in addition to what he called a "Self" and what we call in the believer a "Spirit-led self." First, let's look at *protectors*, the parts of your soul that work to keep you from pain. You're probably familiar with the modus operandi of these hard workers. They're front and center in your life—consistent, persistent, and accustomed to being in charge. When they have healthy boundaries, life's good. When a protector has taken you over, however, you're no longer living from the Spirit-led place within, and you've lost your sense of perspective. You could say you've had a "total eclipse of the heart."[4]

Think of your protectors as falling into one of two categories: *managers* and *firefighters*. Both work tirelessly, though in different ways, trying to protect you from the overwhelming feelings of the more vulnerable parts of your soul. Let's look at managers first.

Managers

Managers are protectors that strive to keep you emotionally safe and prevent more vulnerable parts of you from experiencing harm. They work vigilantly to keep life smooth and predictable. They dutifully get you out of bed in the morning, and in the evening they worry about what didn't get done. They drive you to perform, produce, protect, and please. They push you to stay on top of your game. Managers believe it's impractical for you to get bogged down with emotional pain. At their worst, without healthy boundaries, they can keep you from experiencing emotional growth, deep-down joy, and genuine connection with others.

Managers pursue innumerable activities to try to protect you. Here are some of the most common ones:

- worrying unnecessarily about situations out of one's control
- people-pleasing
- working long hours at the expense of others
- overanalyzing relationships and decisions
- criticizing oneself and others excessively

- exerting extreme control over one's own behaviors or the behaviors of others
- pursuing perfection and refusing to accept human limitations

Firefighters

As valiantly as managers struggle to keep your world free of emotional pain, life has a way of thwarting their best efforts. When you're hurting, another category of protectors, called firefighters, strive to minimize your suffering. We've discussed how managers try to act preemptively. Firefighters, as their name suggests, try to extinguish pain *after* it occurs. These impulsive parts indulge in a lot of whatever feels good, distracting you and tricking you into believing you're handling life well. At their best, firefighters help you care well for yourself so that you effectively manage life's hardships. They remind you when it's time to rest, and they help you unwind. At their worst, if not kept within proper boundary lines, they can lead you down a path of reckless self-indulgence.

Countless firefighter activities numb unwanted feelings. Here are just a few common ways we try to extinguish pain:

- mindlessly surfing the web and escaping through social media
- overexercising, overeating, overcleaning, overspending, oversleeping
- watching entertainment excessively or gambling compulsively
- sexual addiction, excessive daydreaming, or escaping into romance novels
- abusing alcohol or drugs

Are any of these patterns familiar to you?

In addition to managers and firefighters, you also have more vulnerable parts of your soul. Let's call them exiles.

Exiles

We've all experienced some brokenness that we cannot fix . . . some sadness that we cannot undo. We try to forget emotional wounds, but we often deny parts of ourselves in the process. And so parts of us harbor the feelings and insecurities we would rather the world not see. These parts are called exiles because they've been banished or are in hiding. "We try to exile the fallout from dreadful episodes in the past," Schwartz wrote. "But in doing that, we're not only exiling memories, sensations, and emotions; we're also exiling the parts of us that were hurt most by those events."[5]

Exiles are the distressed parts that your managers and firefighters are trying to protect. Voiceless and long neglected, many exiles can be in a state that psychologists call "learned helplessness."[6] They have great need, and they've often yielded their power in counterproductive ways. If not befriended, exiles can cause a host of problems, including phobias or a victim mentality.

The following feelings signal that an exile needs attention:

- shame
- fear
- insecurity
- hurt
- a feeling of worthlessness
- a sense of being marginalized
- a sense of being unseen, unappreciated, or overlooked
- loneliness
- sadness

When it comes to your protectors (managers and firefighters) and exiles, you might think of the stronger parts of you protecting the weaker ones. However, your protectors have limited strategies. Furthermore, they don't understand that "weaker" doesn't mean inferior. As author Andy Crouch astutely noted in his book *Strong and Weak*, "Flourishing requires us to embrace both authority and vulnerability, both capacity and frailty."[7] In the words of the apostle Paul, "the parts of the body that seem to be weaker are the ones we can't do without" (1 Cor. 12:22 NIRV).

Remember Megan from chapter 2? Megan had a strong task manager that had taken over her Spirit-led self. This manager worked tirelessly to protect her from the fears and painful memories she carried. It pushed her constantly to work harder. It said, *You should be a better person! You should be accomplishing more!*

Her task manager was *too close* to her; it had eclipsed her Spirit-led self. Her constant striving had left her feeling weary from overworking and guilty as a result of not spending time with her family. She was sad about feeling emotionally distant from her husband, but she didn't know how to change. Let's see what happened when she gained some distance from her task manager and started leading it from her Spirit-led self.

MEGAN'S PROTECTOR AND EXILE GET TO KNOW HER SPIRIT-LED SELF

In our follow-up session, Megan and I, Kim, further discussed the movie *Inside Out*. I had encouraged her to think of ways her striving task manager was like the character Joy in the movie. Megan was becoming curious about this striving manager that worked so hard.

"What if you affirmed your task manager for how hard it works?" I asked.

"Even the thought of affirming this part of myself, instead of resenting and resisting it, helps me feel calmer," Megan responded.

This manager was trying to motivate her but had lost perspective. It kept her focused on all that she wasn't doing in an attempt to help her do even more. Once Megan's striving task manager began to trust her Spirit-led self, however, it began to relax. It created space for her *exile*—carrying feelings of fear—to receive much-needed attention.

Why did Megan's exile feel fear? The source was easy to trace: When she was young, Megan's dad had been injured and was unable to work, and her mom labored tirelessly to stretch the little money they had. As she grew up, Megan internalized the fear in her mother's eyes—her mother had worried about not being able to pay for heat, food, and medical bills. To escape the stress of her own household, Megan dreamed that she would live in one of the bigger houses down the street. There, she imagined, people were happy all the time.

As an adult, Megan had succeeded in providing for her own family. However, a young, fearful part of her still lingered in her soul in need of care. It constantly ruminated: *What if I fail? What if we lose everything?*

When Megan's fearful exile crept in too close, her task manager would say: *Just work harder.* If she could drive herself hard enough, it thought, she wouldn't have to feel this fear of failure. Because her exile hadn't been healed, her task manager had been working overtime. But Megan soon recognized that overworking wasn't her only option. She had a Spirit-led self far more capable of leading the many parts of her soul to achieve the life she wanted.

"Instead of overworking, what if you were to invite your task manager into times of rest?" I asked. Megan silently contemplated the possibility and, after a moment, said quietly, "I think it would change my life." And she started leading the part to listen to the voice of the Holy Spirit abiding within her, which sounded something like this:

I understand how much you love your family and how badly you don't want to mess up at work. I see how you're conflicted. You're unsure how to balance your priorities. You're afraid that if you drop one ball, everything you're juggling will come tumbling down. I'm with you, and you can trust me to lead and care for you. I love you with an everlasting love. I will never leave you nor forsake you. You are not alone.

As her striving task manager gained trust in God's Spirit within her, it softened. Instead of driving her, it advised her more thoughtfully, saying:

I wonder if my husband would like to talk about how to strengthen our marriage.
I'm starting to catch glimpses of God's peace.
I'm going to slow down and practice listening to him.

As Megan established a comfortable distance from her task manager, her exiled fear moved in closer to her Spirit-led self. There it was witnessed and received the loving attention it needed. Megan started inviting Jesus to be near whenever she felt fear or doubted herself. She practiced listening to his voice saying:

I understand your fear.
I'm with you. You are enough.
I will give you what you need.

Now, when Megan begins to drive herself too hard, she takes a You-Turn. She's able to set gentle boundaries with her task manager and lead it from her Spirit-led self. And she can calm the fearful part of herself. As she integrates the parts of her soul, she's becoming whole. And the same can happen in your life too.

Imagine That!

You can't see the parts of your soul, but God gives you the ability to imagine them. Throughout these pages you'll notice the central role that imagination plays in becoming whole. Especially when sanctified with the presence of the Holy Spirit, the creative mind is a powerful faculty for helping process life experiences. C. S. Lewis described the baptism of his imagination as integral to his spiritual growth. We've found that as clients engage their baptized imaginations, they're more able to access and care for their own complex thoughts and feelings, leading to deeper experiences of inner healing.

Consider tapping into your God-given capacity for coming up with images or figurative language when caring for parts of your soul. You might try naming them as well. Naming helps you call parts of yourself into conscious awareness and bring order to them. When you approach the healing process with creativity, you'll feel empowered to cultivate a mature self-understanding. Imagination helps you develop clarity—increasing your capacity for Spirit-led self-leadership.

WELCOME TO THE FAMILY!

Maybe your life feels chaotic like Megan's. Your *protectors* strive to keep things under control, and your *exiles* clamor for your attention.

Think of these diverse parts of your soul as family members. Imagine a family reunion, where a conversation can be like a ten-way table tennis game. Wrangling relatives into the same room to say grace before a meal can feel like herding wildcats. It helps when everyone has, and responsibly fulfills, a role. Aunt Betty fires up the grill. Cousin Susie picks the music. And Grandpa Lou sets the table. But can you imagine what would happen if Grandpa Lou started a food fight right when Aunt Betty was saying grace? Or if Cousin Susie had to sit in a corner all by herself? Reunions go well only when everyone sets aside personal agendas and cooperates for the good of the whole.

All three kinds of parts within your soul—managers, fire-fighters, and exiles—can cause trouble at any given moment. The good news is they can become like cooperative family members when you develop strong internal boundaries. They can learn to relate to one another well when led by your Spirit-led self.

WHEN A BOUNDARY LINE HAS BEEN CROSSED

So, in any particular moment, how do you know when you could use better boundaries for your soul? How do you know when a protector or an exile is too close or too far? It helps to notice your thoughts and feelings in any given situation. For example:

> *You know it's time for healthier boundaries with a protector when . . .*

you're feeling critical of yourself or others.
you're exhausted from people-pleasing.
you're angry and say hurtful things.
you struggle with making decisions due to worry and fear.
you want to escape.
you feel compelled to make something perfect.
you sense an urgency to fix yourself, or something in your
    life, right away.
you find yourself checking out.

You know it's time for healthier boundaries with an exile when . . .

you ruminate about hurtful memories.
you isolate and withdraw.
you feel like a victim of your circumstances.
you can't stop feeling lonely, even when you're surrounded by
    friends.
you stay in bed too long.
you feel worthless and flooded with shame.

Note: Some (though not all) chronic physical pain can be caused by parts working hard to protect you or by exiled parts in need of healing.[8]

As we described in chapter 2, you know you're leading from your Spirit-led self when you feel curiosity, creativity, and courage. You're cultivating the fruit of the Spirit: love, joy, peace, patience, kindness, goodness, gentleness, faithfulness, and self-control (Gal. 5:22–23). The steps in part 2 show you how to lead your soul from this Spirit-led place.

Even when you're doing so, you'll face difficult situations that stir up emotions like anger, sadness, and envy. Jesus assured us of it, saying, "In this world you will have trouble" (John 16:33). It's best not to ignore these troubling thoughts and feelings. Be present with them and accompany them like a parent leading a young child. Even amid hard circumstances, you don't need to feel overwhelmed. Jesus promised we can experience peace: "But take heart!" he continued, "I have overcome the world."

ALL PARTS ARE WELCOME

We've never met a part of anyone that wasn't earnestly trying to help. Take your anger, for example. It's trying to protect you, so cherish the part of you that feels that way. Consider saying, *I want to thank you, anger, for being there. For helping me to be strong. Without you, I'd be falling apart now. You're a valuable part of me.* Or perhaps, *I can sense your presence with me, sadness. I know it's painful to feel that way. I'm with you, and I love how you make me tenderhearted.*

What thought or feeling needs your care? What doubt or fear is hiding in your soul? Your anger and your fear, and feelings like them, need the loving presence of your Spirit-led self to help them adjust their unhelpful beliefs and strategies. What if you befriended the parts of your soul that carry these troubling emotions and invited Jesus to be near? When you welcome your unwanted thoughts and feelings as valuable members of your internal family, your Spirit-led self can lead those parts of yourself with love.

THE FIVE STEPS OF A YOU-TURN

How do you establish strong boundaries in your soul? In the following chapters, we examine in depth the Five Steps of taking a You-Turn, mentioned in chapter 1:

Step 1: **Focus** on an overwhelming part of yourself.
Step 2: **Befriend** this part you don't like.
Step 3: **Invite** Jesus to draw near.
Step 4: **Unburden** this weary part.
Step 5: **Integrate** it into your internal team of rivals.

These steps show you a new way to be present with striving, fleeing, hurting parts of your soul. You can follow them in the order shown, or you might want to hone in on one step or another. Working through these steps requires courageous authenticity.

And your hard work will produce life-changing results, empowering you to experience God's presence as never before.

So many people feel overwhelmed by their powerful emotions and stubborn ruminations. Ironically, ignoring unruly parts of yourself, such as anger or fear—trying to make these frustrating feelings just go away—causes them to escalate like kids throwing a tantrum. On the other hand, if you befriend them and ask them to give you a little space, they'll relax. The goal is not to eradicate parts of your soul carrying anger, fear, sadness, envy, or shame, but to *lead* them with curiosity and compassion. These parts of you can grow to trust the guidance of your Spirit-led self and take in God's love. The Five Steps offer you a way to care for your internal family so that you can discover wholeness—and as a result peace, joy, and an abundant life.

> **The goal is not to eradicate parts of your soul carrying anger, fear, sadness, envy, or shame, but to *lead* them with curiosity and compassion.**

The Psalms reveal that when he matured spiritually, King David became a leader who brought peace to the war waging within him. He learned the power of reconciling the conflicting parts of himself and prayed to God, "Give me an undivided heart, that I may fear your name." David set his intention: "I will praise you, LORD my God, with all my heart" (Ps. 86:11–12). We've personally adopted this prayer to have a whole heart, and as you read on, know that it's our prayer for you too.

Part II

THE FIVE STEPS OF TAKING A YOU-TURN

He who gets wisdom loves his own soul.

—Proverbs 19:8 NASB

Chapter 4

STEP ONE: FOCUS

You may be ignoring what God is trying to tell you,
running from parts of you that he wants to heal.

—CURT THOMPSON, *ANATOMY OF THE SOUL*

"Suppose one of you has a hundred sheep and loses one
of them. Doesn't he leave the ninety-nine in the open
country and go after the lost sheep until he finds it?"

—LUKE 15:4

WHEN YOU'RE HURTING think of yourself as having a part that's presenting itself for healing. The first step of taking a You-Turn is to *focus* on this part of your soul that's bothering you. We don't mean to focus on it in order to get rid of it—we mean to focus on it and get curious about it. Doing so makes it possible for you to offer the care it needs.

Focusing on a wayward thought or emotion may seem counterintuitive, but how would a surgeon work without first locating an injured part so she can see what she's doing? Locating an overworked or suffering part of your soul also helps you gain perspective. When you realize it's just a part—not the sum total of who you are—your Spirit-led self is beginning to take the lead.

Imagine That!

LIN'S STORY: LEARNING FROM ANGER

"Can you fix him?" Lin asked me, Alison, her eyes peering through blue designer glasses. "I'm *so* angry. Rob is incredibly immature. He never actually listens to me or shares anything meaningful at all. I wish he would just *grow up*."

I took a deep breath and asked carefully, "What would you think about looking more closely at your anger?"

Meeting my gaze, Lin answered, "Isn't *Rob* the one with the problem?"

"I trust that he's hurt you," I replied. "And I also think that your first step in helping your marriage is to focus on what's happening inside of you."

To my relief, Lin accepted my challenge and bravely shifted her attention toward the part of herself that was angry. We learned it came by its feelings honestly. And we learned it had been with her long before her marriage to Rob. To help Lin get to know her anger better, I asked several key questions:

- **Where do you experience your anger physically?** When you feel a strong emotion, pause for a moment and sense where you feel it in your body. Noticing how you experience this part of yourself physically grounds you and helps you understand it. For example, do you experience it in your chest, your shoulders, your head? You may become aware of tension that, once witnessed, might relax and create more space for your Spirit-led self.

  In answer to this question, Lin closed her eyes. "I feel it in my chest, just under my lungs. It's like a tightness that's also making it hard for me to breathe easily." I asked Lin to breathe into the tightness and focus on it with curiosity and compassion.

- **Is there an image that comes to mind when you focus on it?** Often, once you notice the part in your body and start to relax, you can then notice it as an image. You might be surprised that you picture your anger as the color red or as a fire. Or you may become aware of a more detailed image, such as a galaxy of swirling emotions. When you try to visualize the part of you that needs your attention, you access your right brain's creativity and gain insight you might not have gained by analyzing the problem.

  In answer to this question, Lin said that she imagined a smoldering volcano.

- **Is there a thought or belief that comes to mind when you focus on your feeling?** Regardless of whether you notice an image or a thought, or both, the goal is to focus on that part of you with nonjudgmental curiosity, so you can understand it better.

  Lin had an immediate sense of the belief the angry part of her carried: "It thinks I always get the short end of the stick!" she exclaimed, after focusing on the image of the volcano she felt in her chest.

- **How long has this part of you been angry? What are some of its early memories?** You store past events and your responses to them in your implicit memory. You may not be consciously aware of why you respond the way you do. If the troubled part of you shares what it remembers, you can understand better how to address the root cause of the pain.

  In response to being asked about an early memory, Lin remembered a painful season in middle school when her classmates bullied her mercilessly. Her parents were loving but distant emotionally. They worked hard to support Lin and her brother, but they weren't able to help her navigate her tumultuous social life as a teenager. Because she felt lost and disconnected from her peers, Lin's anger had stepped in to protect her from her shame . . . and loyally stood by her side through the loneliness of the next decade. In recent years, her anger was active in her marriage and also showed up when she was on the job, working as a pediatric resident.

But now, sensing Lin's focused attention, this angry part of her soul began to soften. It recognized the presence of her Spirit-led self, a resource she hadn't known was available to her. Connecting to the Holy Spirit within, she became curious about her anger: *I see you there, anger, and I want to get to know you better.* In response, this angry part of Lin's soul began to trust her and share more about its good intentions.

Through our work together, Lin got to know a valuable part of her soul needing attention. She focused on this angry part and connected with it from her Spirit-led self. She noticed where she felt the anger in her body, visualized her anger, identified the key message it believed and a painful memory it held. With time, this angry part of her soul began to transform.

CONSTELLATIONS OF PARTS

Hurting parts of your soul exist in constellations.[1] When you notice one, you can be sure there are more. For example, focusing on your frustration may evoke a sense of guilt. Or paying attention to a critical thought about someone could awaken an inner critic, badgering you about your mean spirit. You might then notice shame, depression, and the desire to escape. Regardless of how many feelings you're experiencing at the same time, the way forward is the same: extend them curiosity and compassion from your Spirit-led self.

When Lin started getting to know the angry part of herself, she noticed more than anger at work. She noticed a sequence of thoughts, each representing another part of herself. Her internal chatter went something like this:

Angry Critic of Rob: *Rob is so selfish!*
Inner Critic: *I shouldn't be so mad at Rob—I'm a terrible wife.*
Shame: *I'm not lovable.*
Depression: *No one will ever love me.*
Escape Artist: *I can't deal with this pain. I wonder what's on television.*

Surrounding Lin's anger were other parts needing her Spirit-led self to show up. To help Lin develop curiosity for her anger, I first asked those other parts of her to give her some space. She needed to stay focused on her anger until she could observe it non-judgmentally and understand why it was so strong.

What does it mean to ask the other parts of yourself to step back? In her bestselling book *Bird by Bird: Some Instructions on Writing and Life*, Anne Lamott addressed this problem of being interrupted by internal chatter. When you're trying to focus, her suggestion is: "Close your eyes and get quiet for a minute, until the chatter starts up. Then isolate one of the voices and imagine the person speaking as a mouse. Pick it up by the tail and drop it into a mason jar. Then isolate another voice, pick it up by the tail, drop it in the jar. . . . Imagine that there is a volume-control button on the bottle. . . . Then turn it all the way down."[2]

You want parts to feel included but not interfere too much. The point is to learn all that you need to know from the original part and later check back with any parts patiently waiting on the sidelines. For those who love math, you might think of this process as "isolating the variable."

Focusing on a protective part, which is what Lin did with her anger, is usually not too hard, because protectors are easy to identify and are typically close to you. But how do you focus on exiles—the lost parts of your soul?

KIM'S STORY: LISTENING TO SADNESS

When I, Kim, was less than a year old, my parents divorced and my biological father moved to Europe. Even at that young age, a part of me absorbed the impact of the loss. Apart from my summer visits with my older sister to see him, he was mostly absent from our lives. He was a fun-loving host during our annual visits, but I don't recall many times that he shared about having weaknesses or difficult emotions. As I grew up, I acutely felt his absence and had a hole in my heart the shape of a charming but distant father.

When I was eight, my devoted mom remarried a caring psychotherapist. I had a loving family, but the subtle, chronic ache in my heart from my father's absence wouldn't subside. A grief-stricken exile was trying to get my attention. I found myself drawn to distant men who, in one way or another, reminded me of my dad. All the while a loyal protector, what I think of as my hardworking reformer, was telling me I must have done something wrong. It thought the best strategy to address my heartache was to try to make me worthier of love.

In my early twenties, as a graduate theology student, by all appearances I was breezing through life. No one would have guessed that internal boundary conflicts threatened to derail me. That is, not until one evening in Vancouver, when my dear friend Jo-Anne and I were visiting in my apartment. I asked her if she had any ideas about how to make my chronic longing go away.

Wise beyond her years, Jo-Anne understood that we can comfort ourselves when we get space from our pain. The psalmist demonstrated such Spirit-led self-leadership when he said, "I have calmed and quieted my soul" (Ps. 131:2 ESV). Jo-Anne handed me a throw pillow from my couch and suggested I hold it as if it were this younger, sad part of myself. The experience helped me realize that my pain was only *one aspect* of my soul—it wasn't and isn't all of who I am. I felt immediate relief, and curiosity. I wanted to find out why this action worked so effectively.

Looking back, I realize that Jo-Anne had taught me how to *focus* on an internal exile, which still felt the experience of abandonment as if it were continuing to happen. The ability to get some space from, and observe, this troubled part, stuck in the past, gave me the perspective I needed in order to pray for it and do something about the grief it was so bravely bearing. To help me focus, I hung on my bedroom wall the last picture taken of my mother, father, sister, and me together. I was the baby perched on my father's shoulders, and we were sitting on the yellow-carpeted stairs of our yellow house with white scalloped trim. I looked at that picture each night and let twenty-five years of sorrow stream down my cheeks as I fell asleep.

My Spirit-led self focused on my exiled part with curiosity, providing the connection it needed. Ironically, when I focused on my sorrow in this way, it took up *less* space in my soul. As the pain subsided, my exile felt relief and, with the Holy Spirit's gentle guidance, eagerly embraced a new point of view. I was able to appreciate more fully the blessings in my life, including many wonderful male friends and mentors, and a devoted stepfather who has become a role model for me. With God's help, I put a gentle boundary around my sorrow, so it could settle comfortably in one chamber of my heart. I felt an affinity with Teresa of Ávila who wrote, "I began to think of the soul as if it were a castle made of a single diamond or of very clear crystal, in which there are many rooms."[3]

WHO AM I, *REALLY*?

As I, Kim, did, you can gain distance from—or *differentiate* from—a suffering part of your soul. Biologists observe how cells differentiate and become more specialized as they divide. Psychologists use the same term when they speak of gaining some distance from another person. Likewise, the process of internal differentiation refers to gaining distance from parts within yourself. You might find yourself asking at times, *Who am I, really?* Differentiating internally empowers you to recognize that a suffering part of you is not *all* of who you are. That realization alone can bring relief from hurting thoughts and feelings.

> You can gain distance from— or *differentiate* from—a suffering part of your soul.

SPEAKING ON BEHALF OF A PART, RATHER THAN FROM IT

Once you've differentiated from a part, you can speak *on behalf of* that part. In other words, you can share with others how you're feeling without doing harm. For example, I, Kim, might have said to my dad, "I'm so grateful that you host me every summer, and a part of me is sad I don't get to see you more often." Likewise, Lin might have said to Rob, "I love you, and a part of me is feeling angry right now." When Lin began to get *curious* about her anger and understand its protective intention, she became able to speak on behalf of this well-intentioned aspect of herself, and to speak more kindly and effectively to Rob.

Speaking *on behalf of* a part, rather than *from* it, is one of the most helpful skills to develop. Doing so

- reminds you that this part of your soul doesn't have the whole story.
- brings the part into contact with the Holy Spirit *before* you express your feelings.
- allows you to speak respectfully to others.
- increases the likelihood that you'll be heard and understood.
- enhances trust between you and God, as well as between you and other people.

Prominent interpersonal neurobiologist Dan Siegel extols the benefits of speaking kindly. His books offer compelling neuroscience research indicating that speaking angrily reinforces the neural pathways in the brain's lower, limbic region, blazing trails of pessimism and dumping neurochemicals associated with anxiety and fear throughout your body—making you feel far worse in the long run.[4] On the other hand, if you speak lovingly on behalf of, rather than *from*, a part of you that is feeling frustrated, you'll feel better.

Extending kindness to another is, in the words of Alexis de Tocqueville, "self-interest rightly understood."[5] When Lin spoke on behalf of her anger—rather than from it—she was improving communication in her marriage and serving both her interests and those of her husband. With better perspective, the demanding part of her that others had deemed an "anger problem" softened and became a trusted adviser that helped her to advocate on behalf of herself in healthy ways.

When you develop the capacity for Spirit-led self-leadership, you communicate more effectively with others and become more of the person you want to be. When the part of you carrying frustration feels heard in a respectful way, it will be more likely to let go of its extreme state and get on board with your attempt to speak kindly. You're able to *advocate* on behalf of parts of your soul when you're relating to them from a comfortable distance.

PURSUING THE LOST SHEEP WITHIN

When walking the earth, Jesus focused on what was lost. Luke 15 records three parables Jesus told about a lost sheep, a lost coin, and a lost son. In each of these stories, the item had tremendous value to the person who had lost it. Exiled aspects of your soul are like the lost sheep, the lost coin, and the lost son: they're alone within your soul yet worthy of being sought after and found. Some of them overwhelm you out of nowhere at times; others hide behind concrete walls of avoidance. Either way, with the help of the Holy Spirit inside you, you can welcome them home.

Can you identify parts of yourself carrying painful thoughts and feelings, parts that hold you back and weigh you down? They may be denied parts of your soul with dreams and abilities, eager to express themselves.

Caring for overworked protectors and hurting exiles can be tricky. They can be stubborn, and they require patience. Your hard work will be rewarded, though. It may be that these very parts you once wished would go away hold the keys to your freedom and joy. Behind their wayward strategies and discouraging tirades, these parts are eager to become your greatest encouragers and advisers.

You pray for others and for God's guidance. Would you extend the same compassion to an injured or straying part of your own soul? Jesus loves lost sheep, and he loves the lost parts of you. You can join with him in finding the lost parts of your soul and bringing them home at last.

FOCUSING ON A PART OF YOURSELF

What's an emotion you're experiencing right now?
Examples:

- *I feel angry.*
- *I feel hurt.*
- *I feel ashamed.*
- *I feel afraid.*
  - Where do you sense this feeling physically? (Sometimes the body remembers what the mind does not.)
  - Is there a thought or image that comes to mind when you focus on it?
  - How far away from you is it? (If it's too close, ask it to step back a little so you can get to know it better.)
  - What is an early memory of this feeling?

Notice without judgment your answers to these questions. You've just taken the step of focusing on one part of your internal family. And what do you do after identifying a troubled part that's either too close or too far from your Spirit-led self? In the next chapter, we'll examine the important step of *befriending* a part of your soul in need.

Chapter 5

STEP TWO: BEFRIEND

But what if this critical person is in your own head?
What if you are the person with the problem?
What if you have met the enemy, and he is you?
—HENRY CLOUD AND JOHN TOWNSEND, *BOUNDARIES*

You prepare a table before me in the presence of my enemies.
—PSALM 23:5

IN CHAPTER 4 we explored ways to *focus* on parts of your soul that need your attention. Often, when you give these parts your close attention, you will notice that you don't like them. In this chapter, we'll show you how to address this internal resistance to unwanted parts of yourself. You'll learn how to strengthen your relationship with your internal protectors, and then the exiles they protect, so that you can grow toward self-acceptance and wholeness.

"Put away your sword," Jesus told a disciple poised to defend him from armed forces sent by political leaders in the Garden of Gethsemane. The king of heaven and earth could have commanded the angels to destroy his enemies and prevent his arrest and execution (Matt. 26:53). Instead, motivated by love, he hung on the cross with nails in his hands and feet until he drew his last breath, saying, "Father, forgive them, for they do not know what they are doing" (Luke 23:34). The cross proved the power of grace.

The cross also underscored one of the most unexpected commands in Scripture: "I'm telling you to love your enemies," Jesus said. "Let them bring out the best in you, not the worst. When someone gives you a hard time, respond with the energies of prayer, for then you are working out of your true selves, your God-created selves" (Matt. 5:43–45 MSG). And what if he meant to extend grace not only to your external enemies but also to the perceived enemies within? You might prefer to get rid of the parts of your soul with these unwanted thoughts and feelings. But is it possible that, with the help of internal boundaries, they might become your greatest allies? Remember: every part of you is valuable and worthy of your compassion, and God loves and wants to do something beneficial through each one.

Think of King David's enemies within: the covetous lover who sent for Bathsheba, the conniving rebel who killed Uriah, the angry commander who struck fear in those who served him (2 Sam. 11). God had given David talent and passion to put to work for great purpose, and yet unruly parts of his soul nearly destroyed his legacy. In the famous Twenty-third Psalm, David wrote that God prepared a table for him in the presence of his enemies. Would God have wanted David to welcome to this table his *internal* enemies—the longing, rebellious, and indignant parts of his soul?

Eventually David befriended his longing exile within and his angry internal protectors and redirected their energy for a higher cause, turning these internal enemies into powerful allies. Are you willing to befriend the parts of your soul you wish would go away—your inner critic, your sadness, your unruly envy? We know it's counterintuitive. And isn't it just like something Jesus would ask you to do? Consider the story of Margaret.

MARGARET'S STORY: UNDERSTANDING
THE MYSTERY OF CUTTING

On a hot summer day, Margaret marched into my, Alison's, office sporting a black, long-sleeve sweatshirt with an image of a giant middle finger on it. I liked her immediately. I've learned that the bolder the armor, the more tender the heart. Twenty-two going on forty, Margaret worked two jobs to make ends meet. She wanted to talk about her boyfriend, John, who would disappear to binge on drugs and women, only to return with gifts and apologies.

I learned during that first session that pointing out the unhealthy nature of her relationship would get us nowhere. Margaret could analyze all of her issues better than I could. She knew John wasn't good for her, but she wouldn't leave him. She was drawn to him like a moth to flame.

When Margaret was five, her father joined a gang. No one had talked much to Margaret about her dad, where he would go, or why he would show up at random and then disappear for years. No wonder John's behavior lured her: there was a young part inside of Margaret's soul that longed for John to redeem her experience with her father by sticking around.

A week later, Margaret arrived for our appointment wearing a tank top revealing the scars on her arms. I knew an invitation when I saw one.

"I'm glad you came back," I said. "I enjoyed meeting you last week."

Margaret glanced at her arms.

"So, you've been cutting?" I ventured.

"Yes," she replied, loosening her armor. "John disappeared. No texts. No calls, nothing." Margaret kept staring at one particularly long cut on her arm: "I felt like I was going to lose my mind. I had to get the pain to stop."

"Can you check in with that part of yourself," I asked, "and tell me if this sounds right: the part that cuts you is protecting you from all that pain in your heart by making you feel physical pain instead?"

Margaret nodded. "I know it's bad. But I can't stop."

Curious if Margaret understood the good intentions of this protective part of her soul, I asked her a question that helps with befriending: "How do you feel toward this part of you that numbs your pain?"

Margaret focused on her cutting part for a moment. "I wish it wasn't there!"

"Could you notice the part of you that doesn't like this powerful cutting part and see if it would be willing to give you some space?"

"Yes," Margaret said. "It's happy that we're talking about the cutting, and I feel calmer just acknowledging that I don't like it."

"That's great, Margaret," I said. "So how do you feel toward the cutting part of you that steps in to numb your pain now?" I wanted to be sure that Margaret was connecting to this part of her soul from her Spirit-led self.

"I'm not as critical of it," she said. "I'm curious about it. It's happy that I understand its good intentions. Most people try to make it go away."

Margaret continued to befriend her internal protector over our next few sessions, and it began to soften. And it also began to trust in the leadership of her Spirit-led self. Simultaneously, it started to show her more of the pain it worked so hard to protect.

"It's showing me a memory," Margaret said a few sessions later. "I was around seven and getting ready to put my little brother to bed. We were supposed to be staying with my dad that weekend, but he hadn't come home. He finally showed up drunk, yelled at me for not having put my brother to bed, threw us both in the car, and drove across the neighbor's lawn to take us to my grandma's. I didn't see him again for three months."

"What did you do then, Margaret? Was there anyone there to help?"

"No," she said. "No one knew. I told myself I had to be strong. My brother needed me."

"So, no one told that little girl that it wasn't her fault? No one helped her see that what was happening was wrong?"

Margaret shrugged. "I was strong," she replied.

"It seems like your cutting part is trying to protect you from feeling all that loneliness and pain," I reflected. "Can you extend it your appreciation for how hard it's been working for you?"

"Yes, I appreciate how much it cares for me. No one has ever understood it. Everyone thinks I'm crazy, but my cutting part actually has kept me alive all these years."

From the moment Margaret connected with her cutting part with compassion from her Spirit-led self, it began to soften. It also showed her the exiled part of her it had been trying to protect. It had been trying, in the only way it knew how, to alleviate the feeling of shame buried inside.

Margaret's cutting part didn't want her to die—it wanted her to live. We identified it as an extreme protector that helped numb her pain. Not until Margaret learned to befriend this hardworking part from her Spirit-led self and appreciate its good intention to help could she get space from it and learn better strategies. And once her exile received the care it needed, her cutting part stopped acting out. Instead, it became a truth teller and a boundary setter, a brave part of her that spoke out when her external boundary lines had been crossed.

You may not cut yourself like Margaret, but we all numb our pain at times, whether with food, drugs, or some other escape, instead of addressing our problems directly. Regardless of their methods of choice, could it be that, like Margaret's cutting part, your internal protectors are actually trying to help?

The idea of befriending internal enemies may counter everything you've been taught about how to handle problematic emotions, but criticizing and rejecting parts of yourself doesn't make things better. What does work is befriending the aspects of yourself you most dislike, so you can win them over. It's about extending yourself hospitality. As Henri Nouwen wrote, "Hospitality . . . means primarily the creation of a free space where the stranger can enter and become a friend instead of an enemy. Hospitality is not to change people, but to offer them space where change can take place."[1] As you extend hospitality to difficult parts of your soul, you create space for internal transformation.

MOVING FROM SELF-CONDEMNATION
TO SELF-ACCEPTANCE

When you focus on, and differentiate from, a troublesome part, ask yourself, *How am I feeling toward it?* Asking yourself how you feel toward a particular part of yourself helps you recognize whether you're leading from your Spirit-led self, which is full of compassion, or from a place of self-condemnation. Healing begins when you connect with this part of yourself from the sacred place within. Your openheartedness toward the part establishes a secure attachment that strengthens over time.

For example, when Margaret focused on her cutting part, she became aware of a critical part that didn't like her cutting part. And you may have a similar experience. If you focus on an envious part, for instance, you may notice a critical part piping up to say, *I'm a terrible person for feeling envy!* Though it may have good reason to be upset by the troubling emotion, your critic needs a gentle boundary. Its condemning attitude toward envy isn't helpful. Let your critic know that you appreciate its concerns, but that you would like to understand and build trust with the part that is experiencing the envy. Once your critic has relaxed, turn your attention back to the original part, and notice what it's like to open your heart to this hardworking member of your internal family.

In taking this pivotal step of befriending a troublesome part of your soul, you're shifting from self-hatred to self-acceptance. Instead of condemning, you're extending the warmth of friendship. Don't hate this part of you; it's been protecting you! Show compassion toward the part of your soul that feels this way. Thank it for being there and for helping you to be strong.

Now let's explore how to befriend protectors and then exiles.

How Change Happens: Myth vs. Truth

Myth: Modifying your thinking is the only way to change.

Truth: Changing your thinking is one important component of growth, and following the Five Steps empowers holistic transformation—cognitively, emotionally, and spiritually.

When you focus with compassion on a troubling part of yourself, you are caring for that part holistically—addressing its unhelpful thoughts *and* the painful emotions it carries. This process involves prayerfully inviting the Holy Spirit to draw close to this specific part of you. Focusing on and befriending a part of yourself in need empowers you to mature in how you think, feel, and relate to God.

BEFRIENDING YOUR PROTECTORS

Think of a protector as a vigilant parent guarding a baby (in the case of manager parts) or trying to comfort that baby (in the case of firefighter parts). Protectors take their roles seriously and are devoted to helping some vulnerable part of your soul in whatever way they know how. That's why you have to gain their trust before they'll relax.

Granted, these parts of you may have developed certain behaviors, emotions, or beliefs that are no longer helpful to you. You may have an internal people-pleaser, competitor, or rigid conflict-avoider. As we mentioned in chapter 3, common protectors include critics, controllers, analyzers, worriers, and parts that have addictions, such as overeating, excessively escaping into entertainment, mindlessly surfing the web, and abusing drugs and alcohol. If you relate to any of these loyal protectors, or others that come to mind, get to know these hardworking parts of your soul and honor their good intentions. Your faithful, diligent protectors need to feel your appreciation before they will trust you to care for the exiles they protect.

Protectors endure harsh criticism from other parts of your internal family—and external family and friends too. When loved ones notice your protectors, their well-intended advice and admonishments rarely help:

"Just relax. You need to slow down."
"Have you prayed about it?"
"Why can't you just stop?"

Comments like these can send your protectors into overdrive, and you end up thinking:

I am *relaxed!*
Don't tell me what to do.
I must be a terrible person because I can't stop.

When challenged, protectors dig in their heels, even more determined to show how indispensable they are to you. Many people admonished Margaret, for example, for cutting herself, but their pleas for her to stop hadn't helped her. Margaret already felt ashamed of her behavior. Furthermore, by trying to control this part of her, well-meaning loved ones only initiated a power play, thereby strengthening her cutting part's resolve to retain control. Like a rebellious teenager, this part of her wanted to be understood and accepted. Once befriended, it relaxed. Then, from her Spirit-led self, Margaret could help this tenacious protector find a new role in her internal family.

Befriending means coming alongside your struggling protectors in a way that helps them find the relief they need. Practice offering these hardworking parts words of affirmation before trying to get them to change. You might say something like:

You're working so hard.
I can understand your worry.
You're deeply caring of others. Thank you for your hard work on
    my behalf.
It makes sense that you're angry.

A friend once told me, Kim, about a time her son was protesting going to school. When she admonished him, he hid under the covers. However, when she said, "Yes, isn't school terrible?" her son replied, "Yeah, it is—let's go!" and hopped out of bed. Because my friend came alongside her son in his fear and frustration, and she reflected, tracked, and joined him in his place of fear, he felt loved and empowered to take on the day. The same approach works for the protesting members of your internal family.

BEFRIENDING YOUR EXILES

When you've befriended internal protectors, they're naturally inclined to give you access to the exiles they protect. These exiles harbor feelings such as self-doubt, loneliness, and fear. Exiles also carry denied and underdeveloped qualities, such as desire, creativity, and ambition.

Be aware that your exiles may have developed subtle victim mantras. Here are a few common ones:

If only he would notice me, then I would feel complete.
I've never had the chance to live my dreams.
Everything is my fault.

Exiles need compassion too. Consider what would happen if you encouraged these parts from your Spirit-led self. For example:

You're doing better than you think.
You matter to me. I hear you. I see you.
I'm here with you now. You are loved.

Connecting with your internal exiles may feel overwhelming at first. They've been carrying burdens and longings for a long time. They have needs, like hungry, neglected children. Margaret had exiled her pain as a result of a major trauma, which you might call "Big-T" trauma. She needed the safety of a counseling office to begin the process of befriending her painful feelings and learning to build strong internal *and* external boundaries. In other cases, you might have exiled a part of yourself as a result of a "small-t" trauma. In those cases, you may be able to befriend your exile and care for its needs on your own. Such was my, Alison's, experience. As a result of a "small-t" trauma, I locked a dreamer part of my soul away until the day it ambushed me, and I had to learn to befriend it.

ALISON'S STORY: CHASING DREAMS

I grew up in a close-knit town in Wyoming with two loving parents and a fun sister. I liked school, was outdoorsy, and had close friends. And I was what you might call a closet dreamer. I had lofty aspirations, a vivid imagination, and strong internal protectors that worked overtime to keep those dreams from proving me a fool.

One dream in particular got the best of me: it centered on the high-stakes world of middle school basketball. And though I was short and not notably athletic, I wanted a spot on that basketball team more than anything on the face of the earth. To help me prepare for tryouts, my parents asked a family friend and the star of our town's high school team to coach me several days a week at our makeshift driveway court. I knew my hard work had paid off when this local basketball legend said to me: "You're good, Alison. You should be on that team."

I was thrilled. The evening of tryouts, my heart was racing. I laced up my brand-new Avia high-tops, shoes only the girls who *knew* they were going to make the team wore, and I ran out onto the court fearful but ready. The coaches paired me with one of the best point guards—and I stood my ground. The crowd gasped as I dribbled past the point guard and scored—winning the one-on-one challenge. *My dream is coming true,* I thought. *Finally, I'll be under the bright lights with all the other girls.*

And I was—for that one night. Because the next afternoon, when we raced into the locker room to see who had made the team, my name wasn't on the list. While my friends hugged and high-fived, I stared down at what had suddenly become a symbol of humiliation—my brand-new high-tops. Trying to hide my shame, I smiled, nodded to my friends, then fled the locker room for the safety of home. In that moment, a part of me developed a powerful new mantra: *Dreaming only ends in heartache. Why bother?* And I stopped chasing dreams, for at least a decade.

Instead, I learned to smile and nod from the bleachers and then hide myself in books. This smile-and-nod part worked well as a protector—keeping the pain of unrealized dreams away by telling me, and everyone around me, that I was "just fine."

My dream to live boldly didn't overwhelm me back then. It hid far away, in a distant chamber of my soul, where it was staging a coup—unbeknownst to me. The rebellion occurred years later on a weekend in May, one morning after I had turned in my dissertation proposal. I had been smiling and nodding my way through a demanding year, working long days as a student adviser to put myself through graduate school. My best friend had married, and I hadn't been on anything close to a date since I had accidentally danced with a groomsman at her wedding the prior summer. (My dating life had stalled when I started believing the *dreaming only ends in heartache* mantra.) That evening I found myself with no work to distract me. None of my students were in crisis, and my writing deadline had been met. I sat alone in the silence of my apartment, aware of the bright sunlight filling up the room, and all I could feel was emptiness inside. In that moment, fed up with the loneliness that comes from being emotionally cut off and buried in books, my exiled dreams overwhelmed me in the form of a panic attack.

The onslaught of overwhelming emotion was a shock to my smile-and-nod protector, who protested the arrival of this unwanted exile, saying, *You are fine. You help people. You work hard. Everything is under control.* But this dreamer part, buried for years, refused to be silenced: *I AM NOT FINE!*

I called my sister, who encouraged me to become curious about this unwanted dreamer. And as I did, the anxiety soon subsided. I listened to it for the next few months, and it said: *I'm tired of hiding away in fear. I'd like a break from the books. I'd love to do something creative. I want to learn how to act!* I was surprised by its consistency—acting was another dream I'd had as a child, but after the basketball fiasco, I hadn't given it the time of day. But now I began to make friends with it and asked my smile-and-nod protector to get on board. I set aside my studies, found a job in Los Angeles, and signed up for an acting class. It was the first time since the basketball tryouts that I had let such an outsize dream become a priority.

Acting was a challenge. And initially I wasn't very good at it. One night my acting teacher said with loving sincerity, "I don't think I've ever met someone with so much energy and knowledge with so little awareness of herself." I couldn't even smile and nod, because another part, my shaming inner critic, reared up, saying, *Who do you think you are? You're making a fool of yourself.*

But this time was different. Something inside, that I now know to be my Spirit-led self, stayed present to the painful feeling, and so I was able to befriend it too: *I see you there in front of me, shaming critic, and you're trying to keep me from making a fool of myself. I get that this bold dream feels uncomfortable to you. Let's hang in there and see what happens.*

It took me a solid year before I got the hang of acting. It was worth it, though, to get to know the dreamer part I had exiled. My dreamer part was willing to work hard. It craved excellence. It wanted me to live courageously—whether that meant I made the team, aced the character, or went down trying. It turned out this dreamer part was more resilient than other parts of my soul thought.

And my hard work befriending the dreamer in me paid off—not only in helping me learn to act, but in other areas of my life. I returned to finish my doctoral program and I met Kim, who started telling me about the concept of befriending parts of the soul. I began to integrate this new approach with my studies and could now pursue my vocation wholeheartedly. I turned dreams into realities in my dating life too. Shortly thereafter I met and married a man who loved the dreamer in me.

EXTENDING GRACE

As I, Alison, did, we all try to avoid painful, uncomfortable feelings, such as desire, anger, shame, fear, and sadness. But life's too short to keep important parts of ourselves locked away because of the burdens they carry. If a part of your soul is tugging at you, focus on it and befriend it. Cultivate curiosity and learn what it needs.

Just as it's important for a baby to have secure attachment with her mother, your exiles need secure attachment with your Spirit-led self.[2] Through the warmth you extend them, you can nurture this vital attachment. As you do, watch in wonder as your exiles mature, find their voices, and step out of the shadows and into the light.

The key to keeping extreme thoughts and feelings in check is not to get rid of them, but to extend grace and guide them from your Spirit-led self. Being gentle with yourself brings you peace. As you attune empathetically to your extreme thoughts and feelings, they'll become more willing to settle harmoniously into your internal family.

You'll know that you have befriended parts of your soul when your Spirit-led self has taken the lead. That is, when you have perspective and the ability to lead the disparate parts of your soul compassionately, creatively, and courageously.

As Jesus said, befriend your enemies. Love them. "Let them bring out the best in you, not the worst. When someone gives you a hard time, respond with the energies of prayer, for then you are working out of your true selves, your God-created selves" (Matt. 5:44–45 MSG). As you befriend the parts of your soul that you've dismissed as troublesome, or downright bad, and transform them into your allies, you become more whole. You gain freedom from the burdens you've carried, and you build trust internally and with God. You live with greater confidence and can build greater intimacy with others too.

> **As you befriend the parts of your soul that you've dismissed as troublesome, or downright bad, and transform them into your allies, you become more whole.**

BEFRIENDING A PART OF YOUR SOUL

See if you can identify an internal protector right now. What is it feeling?

Examples:

I feel angry.
I feel critical.
I wish I could escape.

How do you feel *toward* that feeling?

Examples:

I'm mad at myself for feeling that way.
I feel guilty about how I responded.

I'm afraid the feeling will never go away.
I don't know what I would do without it.

If you recognize anything except curiosity and compassion, then you've identified another part of your soul. See if this part will give you some space to allow you to focus on your original response.

Connect to the original part from your Spirit-led self and extend it your compassion, as you would to a friend. Consider the following questions:

- Is this part of you protecting a deeper pain or desire?
- Can you befriend this exiled part?
- What more do these parts of your soul want you to know?

If you completed the exercise, you've befriended a protector and an exile. Now we're wondering—is Jesus near these parts of your soul? Are they hearing what he has to say?

Chapter 6

STEP THREE: INVITE

The windows of my soul I throw wide open to the sun.
—John Greenleaf Whittier

Draw near to God, and he will draw near to you.
—James 4:8 (esv)

Imagine your clamorous crew of internal family members at a church service. Your managers, busy trying to survive, might dutifully sit through a sermon, but they believe they have more important things to do than actually listen and apply the lesson. Your firefighters, distracting you from pain, keep looking for the exits and planning their next escape. And your exiles in hiding might feel the farthest from God. Does it sometimes seem these feelings are in charge? Although you earnestly desire to live at peace with God, are you losing the war within your soul?

How do you care for those parts of yourself that are angry, acting out, and afraid? We've discussed the benefits of *focusing* and *befriending*. The next step is *inviting* Jesus to be near a struggling part of your soul. As an example, let's consider a client named Jenna.

Imagine That!

Scripture is filled with figurative language: God told Abraham that his descendants would be as numerous as the stars. David's soul was a deer panting for water. Solomon's banner was love.

Jesus often used figurative language. For example, he invited his followers to imagine how the kingdom of God is like yeast that leavens bread, how a judge might rule if hounded by a persistent widow, and how a father might respond if his prodigal son returned home. When explaining to his disciples what was to come, he described himself as a kernel falling to the earth to bear fruit and as a temple that would be rebuilt in three days. When you engage your imagination, you're participating in a rich creative tradition.

JENNA AND HER TALL PILE OF BOOKS

Jenna walked into my, Kim's, quiet home office at a New York cadence. She was on a mission to escape her loneliness. Though she wanted to experience the peace of God she had learned about at church, it had eluded her for years. Considering all the great sermons she had heard, she couldn't figure out why she was still plagued by loneliness. When she explained her conundrum, I asked her to pause, engage her imagination prayerfully, and focus on what she was experiencing. After a moment, Jenna said she pictured herself standing next to a towering stack of unread books. The books, she said, represented all the sermons she had heard. Instead of letting the words reach her heart, some angry part of her soul was tossing the sermons on top of the growing stack. Embracing the idea that Jenna's soul is made up of firefighters, managers, exiles, and a Spirit-led self, we soon came to think of this angry part as a well-meaning firefighter, trying to extinguish her loneliness and numb her pain.

Jenna had grown up in a rigid household in which she struggled to be heard. She had been an obedient daughter, the only one of her siblings who didn't rebel. Watching as her parents fought with her outspoken siblings, Jenna remained silent. In fact, whenever she would try to talk to her domineering father, she would be overwhelmed by fear and would cry. As a result, she ended up with a lonely exile that had never found its voice.

As Jenna and I worked together over several sessions, we further explored her internal boundary problems: She had a dutiful manager that kept her quiet and made her go to church, as she had been taught to do. In addition, her angry firefighter would think, *Fine! I'll go to church, but I'm not going to listen to anything the preacher says.* Both of these warring protectors had eclipsed her Spirit-led self. She attended church faithfully but tuned out the message. All the while, her exiled loneliness, desiring to have a voice, continued to weigh her down. Jenna needed to get some distance from her dutiful manager and her angry firefighter so this lonely exile could get the care it needed.

To help Jenna establish healthier internal boundaries, we decided to see if her angry firefighter would be willing to step back. She had already befriended it, thereby gaining its trust. So we now turned to the step of *invite*.

"Jenna, as you imagine your angry, resentful part, where does Jesus seem to be in relationship to it?" I asked. "Is he close or far?"

"It's as if I can barely see him," she replied softly. "He's standing in the distance. I wish he would come closer."

As she stayed focused on her angry part, we simply invited

Jesus to draw near. A few minutes later, after waiting in silence, Jenna described a scene she envisioned: "He's there with my anger now, and he's putting his hand on its shoulder." A sense of peace came over Jenna as she took in the presence of the One written about in her stacks of books. Gradually, Jenna's anger softened as it got to know Jesus in a new way. As it did, her exiled loneliness gained access to the caring, listening presence of her Spirit-led self. And her dutiful manager relaxed its controlling grip.

Jenna's story reminded me of something that happened after Jesus' resurrection. Jesus was walking on the road to Emmaus with two of his followers who were discussing all that they knew of him while completely unaware that he was right there, present with them. In fact, even after Jesus explained to them that the scriptures they were discussing were about him, they still didn't understand that he was the Messiah whom they so longed to see (Luke 24:27). Likewise, Jenna had been studying about God for years at church, but parts of her hadn't been connecting to his living presence within her. But now, after encountering him, Jenna wholeheartedly *wanted* to go to church and to learn about the God who loves her through and through.

Are parts of you far from God and in need of his loving presence? If so, you're not alone. Jesus spent time with all types of people, including the sanctimonious ones trying to keep everyone in line, the straying ones breaking the rules, and the suffering ones who lived on the fringes. Interestingly, these three groups from the Gospels sound a lot like the managers, firefighters, and exiles that make up your internal family. When these rivaling parts of your soul have not drawn near to Jesus, you can imagine what happens: Your sanctimonious managers beat up on the straying and suffering parts. Your straying parts start going rogue and the suffering ones grope around for the emergency *Help!* button.

Although we can see patterns in Jesus' actions in the Gospels, his life defies formulas. As you invite Jesus to draw near the sanctimonious, straying, and suffering parts of your soul, you might be surprised by how he responds to each one. One of the most common features in the Gospels is the element of surprise.

SANCTIMONIOUS, STRAYING, AND SUFFERING PARTS

The Sanctimonious

Throughout the Gospels, Jesus interacted frequently with the religious leaders who knew every letter of the law—and who, when they had mastered laws, created more. They excelled at keeping up a positive appearance while masking their insecurities and weaknesses (Luke 11:43–44). Jesus expressed his desire to be close to them when he quoted Isaiah, saying, "These people honor me with their lips, but their hearts are far from me" (Mark 7:6).

These sanctimonious leaders resemble our moralistic managers. Consider some of their common beliefs:

Legalists: *All that matters is that rules get followed.*

Judgers: *I do a better job of following rules than others I know.*

Prideful Doers: *God loves me because I'm so good at getting things done.*

Perfectionists: *If every hair isn't in place, God won't love me.*

Prima Donnas: *I deserve special treatment.*

People-Pleasers: *I'm nice and help people in need, even when it kills me!*

Pushy Point-Makers: *I'm going to staple the truth to your forehead!*

These well-meaning parts work to keep you and others on the straight and narrow, but they sometimes get too close and take over your Spirit-led self.

Too Close or Too Far?

If your moralistic managers are too close, you risk exiling parts of yourself that are suffering. These hardworking parts might be downright combative at times, though they are trying to help. They work to maintain your reputation—with others and with God. They're fighting to keep your faults and limitations far from view. These parts often believe they're speaking on behalf of God, when in fact they sometimes keep you from establishing a more meaningful relationship with him.

On the other hand, if these managers are too far away, you may not do those good, kind things that show you are a child of God. Although the Gospels record that Jesus had the toughest words for the sanctimonious, he also said to "let your light shine before others, that they may see your good deeds and glorify your Father in heaven" (Matt. 5:16). It was helpful, for example, that Jenna's dutiful manager kept her going to church, because it was there that she learned about the Holy Spirit.

For these parts of your soul to get to know Jesus better, often you have to ask them to step back so your Spirit-led self can lead. You can then invite Jesus to draw near to these hardworking parts and find out what they need. Remember how, in Genesis, God rested and told us to do the same? Your moralistic managers don't always fully understand the notion of rest. As you invite Jesus to be near them, they'll begin to understand that stepping back doesn't mean lowering their standards—it means that, to be most effective, you need to get rest, do what you can, and maintain humble perspective.

Jesus desires to befriend your sanctimonious managers. When

a religious leader, Nicodemus, sought him out late at night, Jesus befriended him. In fact, Jesus shared with Nicodemus the hope-filled message that he had come to save, not condemn, the world (John 3:17). In response, Nicodemus became Jesus' loyal friend, one of two who prepared his crucified body for burial and laid him in the tomb (John 19:39–40). Jesus wants to put your sanctimonious managers to work for his, and your, highest good.

The Straying

Jesus also spent time with people whom the religious leaders called "sinners," those whose sin was more obvious. These were the people who committed adultery (John 8:1–11), rebelled (Luke 15:11–32), cheated, stole (Luke 19:1–10), and routinely stepped out of line. In fact, Jesus' followers and the pious teachers of his day rebuked him for dining with those considered sinners and for letting them touch him (Mark 2:15–16; Luke 7:36–39). Notably, it was a woman four times divorced—and from Samaria, a place equivalent to "the wrong side of the tracks"—whom Jesus honored by disclosing his true identity. This woman at the well said to him, "I know that Messiah . . . is coming. When he comes, he will explain everything to us." He responded, "I, the one speaking to you—I am he" (John 4:25, 26).

Typically, Jesus didn't have harsh words for sinners. Instead, he said, "It is not the healthy who need a doctor, but the sick. I have not come to call the righteous, but sinners" (Mark 2:17). He often befriended them, forgave them, and *then* called them to change: "Neither do I condemn you. . . . Go now and leave your life of sin" (John 8:11).

These straying "sinners" sound like our firefighter parts. Consider some common examples of their beliefs:

Prodigals: *I'm bored with living God's way. I want to play by my own rules for a while.*

Rabble-Rousers: *God, you rain on my parade! I'm going to liven things up, and it'll feel so good!*

Slackers: *What does it really matter, anyway? You'll forgive me later.*

Skeptics: *You don't make sense to me, God. I'm going to look for another path that does.*

Mavericks: *Laws were made to be broken!*

Escape Artists: *I don't feel like sticking around. I'm outta here!*

These well-meaning firefighters work to numb your frustrations with life, the church, and God. Often, in doing so, they hijack your Spirit-led self.

Too Close or Too Far?

Rebellious firefighters struggle to extinguish your pain. If they're too close, you risk missing out on the life Jesus has in store for you. They can lead you away from God and into trouble. Sometimes, as with Jenna, they do so insidiously by luring you to "check out," when what you really need is to face your pain. If these parts get extreme, you could end up in a heap of rubble, regrets, and ruined relationships.

On the other hand, if your firefighters are too far you may miss out on the life-giving pleasures and exciting adventures that God created for you to enjoy. You may also miss opportunities to operate effectively outside of your comfort zone. Jesus demonstrated a willingness to buck the system when he healed a man on the Sabbath (Mark 3:1–6). Your rambunctious firefighters, when led by Jesus, can point out flaws in oppressive, legalistic systems.

Firefighters have the opportunity to be forgiven greatly; where sin is great, God's grace abounds. Once, a hard-living woman washed Jesus' feet with her tears. "Her many sins have been forgiven—as her great love has shown. But whoever has been forgiven little loves little," Jesus said (Luke 7:47). When shown mercy, your inner skeptic may develop compassion for those who struggle to have faith. Your returning prodigal part may feel tenderness toward those fighting to overcome the ravages of their own dangerous rebellions. Having healthy boundaries, these parts can extend mercy and forgiveness to others with the mercy they themselves have received.

Embrace your loyal firefighters, even if they feel like your internal enemies. These well-meaning parts of your soul need to be redirected, not berated. If you find that you're shutting out God or being tempted to sin, listen to that part, and get to know it. Most importantly, invite Jesus to be near it too.

The Suffering

Jesus also encountered many people who were suffering. He didn't blame the suffering, nor did he marginalize them. Instead, he encouraged them, helped them, and treated them with respect. And in many cases, he healed them. For example, he healed ten men slowly dying from incurable disease (Luke 17:12–16); a woman who, after twelve years of suffering, touched his robe (Matt. 9:20–22); a man who could not walk (Mark 2:12); a man who had been blind since birth (John 9:6–7); and a young boy on his deathbed (John 4:50), to name a few.

In each of these cases, Jesus asked the suffering person to do something before being healed: "Get up, take your mat and go home" (Mark 2:11); "Go back home. Your son will live!" (John 4:50 NLT); and "Wash in the Pool of Siloam" (John 9:7). And he wants to empower the suffering parts of *you*.

The suffering characters we encounter in the Gospels sound like our exiles. When our managers and firefighters know Jesus is near, they're willing to relax and make room for these hidden, hurting parts of us to emerge. Consider some of their most common beliefs:

Unworthiness: *God doesn't truly love me.*
Shame: *I'm damaged and beyond God's forgiveness.*

Insecurity: *I'm not as important as other people. Why would God bother with me?*

Doubt: *Does God really care? Why would he let me suffer so much?*

Bitterness: *I'm angry at God because of what he has let happen to me and to those I love.*

Too Close or Too Far?

You may be unaware of the heavy burdens your suffering exiles carry—they may be too far away. If you neglect your wounded-by-religion exiles and hide your brokenness and frailties from God, you risk being passive in your faith and fail to "get up and walk." On the other hand, if your suffering exiles are too close, you may be overwhelmed by your pain. Whether too close or too far, your exiles need the healing presence of your Spirit-led self.

Invite Jesus to draw near, and you might notice his invitation for them to take leaps of faith that seemed impossible before. In his presence, these suffering parts of you find comfort and healing. With healthy boundaries, exiles can transform into beautiful aspects of your humanity—channels of empathy and grace.

Jesus loves every part of who you are—your sanctimonious managers, straying firefighters, and suffering exiles too. When your protectors become prayerful and your exiles find strength, your internal life will become more integrated and peaceful. You'll enjoy more compassion for others and an ever-deepening intimacy with God. All parts of you are valuable and well-intentioned at their core, even when they're making things worse. Learn which parts of your soul to bring in closer and which to ask to step back. Connect to each from your Spirit-led self. When you love and guide them, they'll be willing to adjust their strategies.

Here's an example of how one man, Tom, developed healthy boundaries with his pride.

TOM'S STORY: WORKING WITH PRIDE

"Any woman would be thrilled to be married to me," Tom proclaimed to me, Kim, running his hand through his slick black hair during our first session. Ann, his wife, was not impressed. When I asked them to face each other, she didn't budge.

The last straw for Ann had come a few weeks earlier: She had shared with friends over dinner that she and Tom were about to see a marriage counselor. "It's cheaper to keep her!" Tom had joked. No one laughed but Tom.

Tom was manly, ill-mannered, and mad at God, though he didn't know it. As we further explored their marital conflict, he complained, "After all I've done for God, he gives me a wife who doesn't respect me?" Tom continued to list in detail the things he had done right: "I work hard. I'm a faithful spouse. I'm so much better than so many men out there. Don't I deserve some respect for all I do day after day?"

Occasionally, I could see glimmers of Tom's true heart. But most of the time, his entitled manager crowded out his Spirit-led self. From the perspective of this powerful protector, the only problems in the marriage were Ann's ingratitude and lack of interest in physical affection.

This prideful part needed to step back and gain perspective. I knew that wouldn't happen until Tom befriended it. During our next session, I started by affirming Tom's good deeds: "I see how hard you're working, and it's wonderful that you do so many things for God," I said. Tom responded well to my praise and shared more details about what a good job he was doing for "the man upstairs."

Next, I led Tom on a deep-dive exploration to discover what was motivating his prideful manager. "How do you feel toward this part of yourself that's so proud of the kind of husband you are?" I asked.

"I feel great about it!" he replied without hesitation.

"Tom, what if this virtuosity you appreciate about yourself might be what's so difficult for Ann to tolerate? Is it possible that Ann might want to get to know the parts of you that *aren't* doing so well?"

For once, Tom was speechless.

Gradually, he was able to focus on the pride that was eclipsing his Spirit-led self. As he differentiated from this prideful part, he sensed God's affirmation of its hard work: *I see you; I get you.* And he became open to inviting Jesus to be near it too. This recalcitrant part of Tom's heart began to soften, giving him access to the more tender parts of his soul that needed Jesus to be near.

As we continued to work together, I wanted to find out more about what Tom's pride had been protecting. "How long has that feeling of not getting rewarded for your hard work been with you?" I asked. Tom recalled how his father, a minister, had been consumed by the needs of his parishioners. At times he had neglected to acknowledge or validate Tom's hard work at school. An exiled part of Tom, carrying the pain of neglect, was stuck in the past.

"What does this neglected part of your soul want us to know?" I asked.

"It feels like a gnawing sense of worthlessness," he replied. "It's wondering what was more important than me."

I suggested Tom pause, close his eyes, and see if he could sense God's presence.

"Is Jesus near the neglected part of you?" I asked.

"He's near," Tom said, his bluster subsiding. "He's telling me that my Father in heaven loves me."

Tom began to see more clearly that his prideful manager had taken over and kept him from facing his pain of feeling unimportant. He also began to realize that Ann felt closer to him when he was transparent with her. She didn't want him to be perfect. She wanted to know all of who he was.

Many of us have been taken over by powerful internal protectors that cloud our view of reality. Managers, in particular, convince us that we're self-sufficient and entitled to rewards. When these well-meaning parts obscure our Spirit-led self, we begin to see ourselves as the center of the world, and we lose sight of God. These parts of us don't always want to invite Jesus to be near, because that would mean giving up control.

Tom bravely befriended the parts of himself that needed to be healed. Then he invited Jesus to be near them. In the months that followed, Tom and Ann restored their marriage, and they worked on restoring Tom's relationship with their children too.

HOW TO FIND A PART THAT'S FAR FROM JESUS

So, how can you grow closer to Jesus? You might start by noticing what happens when you engage in spiritual disciplines, such as prayer and worship.

Can you identify a sanctimonious manager? For example, if you notice a lot of *shoulds* in your mind, such as, *You should be praying longer.* Or, *you shouldn't be feeling distracted or angry*, you can bet these messages are coming from a manager that's trying to help you rather than from God. Jesus' voice, although authoritative, is never shaming. Pray for that part of your soul that has internalized a critical spirit—it needs your care. Assure that part of you that you understand its concern; your true desire is to connect authentically with Jesus.

Consider, also, how your straying firefighters respond when you turn your mind to God. For example, you might notice a part nodding off, distracting you with daydreams, or luring your attention with your favorite escape. Focus on and befriend these well-meaning firefighters and ask them to give you some space so you can keep your eyes on God.

As your protectors step back, you can invite Jesus to draw near the suffering parts of your soul most in need of his care. You might become aware of a suffering part that's feeling far from God or doubting his goodness. Focus on and befriend this suffering part, and witness it from your Spirit-led self: *I see that you're lonely. I'm here with you.* As you turn your attention to these struggling parts, you're developing a richer, more intimate relationship with God.

Learning to welcome every part of your soul can be challenging. When I, Alison, first befriended my exiled dreamer part, my sanctimonious smile-and-nod protector wasn't happy: *It's selfish to consider your own dreams; you should only think of others.* But as it gave me some space, I was surprised to find that Jesus didn't want to banish my exiled dreamer. Instead, he invited it into a place of honor in my soul and helped me integrate it into the rest of my internal family. I realized that my sin had not been in having a part of me that desired creativity and sometimes out-of-the-box expression; my sin was in rejecting that God-given part of myself

Beware of Imposter Religious Parts

Be aware that sometimes when you try to connect with Jesus, you actually may be connecting with a religious, Jesus-like part. You know this is the case when the "Jesus" you feel like you're encountering is shaming you or has no power. In your imagination the part may imitate Jesus, though it's not really him. This part may have fears of change or losing its role, so it poses as Jesus. If a well-meaning part like this shows up as you start to pray or participate in a worship service, ask it to step back so that you can connect with the living God. The true Jesus always speaks authoritative words of hope and truth that will change your life.

> When you spend time with God, don't leave your unwanted thoughts and feelings at the door. Instead, *befriend* them—and *invite* Jesus to be near them too.

and trying to lock it out in the cold. Jesus wanted to embrace the dreaming part of me and make it even more beautiful in my soul for his glory.

When you spend time with God, don't leave your unwanted thoughts and feelings at the door. Instead, *befriend* them—and *invite* Jesus to be near them too. Start with one thought or feeling that's troubling you. You may be weary of doing good, like Jenna. Or you might struggle with pride, like Tom. In the same way that Jenna introduced Jesus to her anger, Tom began to understand his pride. Jenna and Tom both learned to practice Jesus' presence, and as a result, they've found freedom and joy.

OPENING THE WINDOWS OF YOUR SOUL TO THE SON

As you grow closer to God, it may be that you don't need to pray more than you're already praying—it may be helpful simply to pray in a new way. Interceding on behalf of a specific part can enrich the time you already spend with God. Invite Jesus to be near a hurting part, and hold it up to the light. Paying attention to the state of your soul opens you up to receive the gifts God wants to give to the parts of you most in need of grace.

Imagine a friend standing outside your door, bearing gifts chosen just for you. Imagine he's eager to speak words of affirmation and meet you in your pain. Wouldn't you let him in? This step of invitation involves guiding each part of your soul—the sanctimonious, the straying, and the suffering—to open the door, open their arms, and receive treasures from God.

You want to be genuine inside and out, true from start to finish. Journeying toward wholeness involves inviting Jesus to be *with* your inner legalist, rabble-rouser, and the lonely orphan within. Invite every part of your soul to God's table and discover, along with the psalmist, that "in [his] presence there is fullness of joy" (Ps. 16:11 ESV).

Set an intention with yourself: the next time you listen to a sermon, study Scripture, engage in worship, or start to pray, consider how you might include and care for a struggling part that inevitably came along. Here are some ways you could invite Jesus to be near the part you've identified:

- Pray for this part of yourself as you would pray for a close friend in need.
- Notice this part of your soul when you worship God. Is it able to receive his gifts?
- Read Scripture over this part of you and tune in to what it feels.
- Take a weekly Sabbath, or time to rest, and spend time getting to know this part of yourself that's presenting itself for healing.

As you invite Jesus into what you are experiencing right now, you'll become more aware of his constant presence. As the Carmelite Brother Lawrence wrote in his seventeenth-century classic work *The Practice of the Presence of God*, "I keep myself retired with Him in the depth of the center of my soul as much as I can; and while I am so with Him I fear nothing; but the least turning from Him is insupportable."[1]

In her inspiring book *Soul Feast*, Marjorie Thompson wrote that spirituality involves "conscious awareness of . . . the work of the Spirit in us."[2] And in *Celebration of Discipline*, Richard Foster observed, "By themselves the Spiritual Disciplines can do nothing;

they can only get us to the place where something can be done. They are . . . the means by which we place ourselves where [God] can bless us."[3] Our religious activities, or spiritual disciplines, on their own don't change us—they create an environment in which growth can occur.

INVITE JESUS TO BE NEAR

Is there a problem in your life that's requiring your attention like a light on your car's dashboard? Identify any sanctimonious, straying, or suffering part that might be keeping you from Jesus. For example, are you feeling critical toward someone? Are you frustrated with a spouse, sibling, or child? Are you tempted to sin in some specific way? Is a part of you struggling with loneliness or sorrow?

Focus your attention on that feeling. Notice how that part responds, in particular, when you practice your spiritual disciplines, such as prayer, worship, or Bible study. When you focus on that part of yourself, what else do you feel? Pay attention to this response. Unless it's a feeling like curiosity or compassion, you've encountered another part. See if that second part will step back just a little bit to allow you to focus on your original response.

Return to that original part of yourself with curiosity and ask it:

- Is Jesus near?
- If not, would this part like to invite Jesus to be near? Does it have any fears and concerns? Can it tell those things to him?
- Ask Jesus if he wants to say, do, or give the part anything in response.

STEP THREE: INVITE

You've just taken a step toward inviting Jesus to draw near to a part of yourself that may have been distant from him. In doing so, you're leading your internal family in partnership with God. Notice what it feels like to invite Jesus to be with a part of your soul that has never before known the power of his love.

Whether you feel as if you're shining like a stained-glass window or broken like shards of glass, beautiful things happen when you invite Jesus to be near parts of your soul in need. The more you know him, the more you reflect his goodness. Now we're wondering—do the weary parts of your soul have anything they need to *unburden*? If so, in the following chapter you'll find encouragement and help with this important step.

Chapter 7

STEP FOUR: UNBURDEN

Gonna lay down my burdens
Down by the riverside.
—African American spiritual

Give all your worries and cares to God,
for he cares about you.
—1 Peter 5:7 (nlt)

Do you ever feel as though you've tried everything to get rid of painful thoughts and feelings, but they simply won't budge? Guilt. Bitterness. Anger. Fear. Have they resolutely resisted your most heroic efforts? If so, know this: you can be free from such heavy burdens. Listen and get to know your heart. Jesus doesn't promise to take your problems away, but he does want you to bring your worries to him and find rest for your soul (Matt. 11:28–30).

In this chapter, you'll learn to identify the parts of yourself that are carrying heavy burdens from the past. When you get to know these various dimensions of your soul through *focusing*, *befriending*, and *inviting*, you'll discover that they often want to *unburden*. And God always has good things for them in return. Here's an example from the life of a woman named Nicole.

NICOLE'S STORY: UNBURDENING FALSE GUILT

"I love my family, and I want my mom to be a part of my kids' lives," Nicole told me, Alison, during our first meeting. "But I feel so much guilt. My mom would spend every second with us if she could. And I feel terrible telling her no."

Nicole felt she was abandoning her mother by setting boundaries on their time together. She kept thinking, *How can I be happy while Mom feels left out?* As we began to work together with this guilt-tripping manager part, Nicole focused on it, befriended it, and began to learn more about its false belief: *I'm selfish if I say no.* For reasons we would soon discover, this part of Nicole worked diligently to make sure she constantly took care of others.

"What is this loyal part of you afraid might happen if it doesn't do its job?" I asked.

"I'll become selfish if I don't put my mother first," Nicole replied. "She relies on me to take care of her."

"It seems important to this guilt-tripping part of you to care well for others. That's an honorable desire," I reflected, affirming the good intention of her internal protector.

As I spoke, Nicole began to cry; a young exile jumped in. "God won't love me anymore," Nicole said softly. "If I stop taking care of my mom, I'll lose his love." With all evidence to the contrary, a young part of Nicole, lost within the caverns of her soul, had been believing this lie.

When Nicole was young, her single mom had struggled with illness and loneliness. She looked to Nicole to help keep the household running—more than is healthy for a young child to do. Buried inside, Nicole's tender exile developed a false belief about herself: *I'm worthy of God's love only when I care for others.* From Nicole's Spirit-led self, she began to connect with this vulnerable part.

"Does this part want to unburden that belief?" I asked.

Seizing the opportunity to release this exhausting belief, Nicole nodded.

Knowing that Nicole's faith was important to her, I asked, "Is Jesus near?"

Nicole paused for a few moments, staying connected to this young part of herself.

"Yes, he's letting me know he loves me unconditionally, not because of what I do for others. He's letting that little girl know that it wasn't her job to care for Mom—that's his responsibility."

In her imagination, Nicole could see her younger self releasing this burden of responsibility to Jesus. Taking in his love, she extended her hands toward him and, one by one, handed over her worries about letting others down.

"I feel lighter," Nicole said.

Nicole's process of unburdening started when she *focused* on and *befriended* her internal guilt-tripper that told her she had to earn God's love by taking care of others. As this hardworking protector experienced the compassion of her Spirit-led self, it showed her the exile it had been protecting and the burdensome belief this exile had been carrying—that God's love depended on how well she cared for others. Now, Nicole could *invite* Jesus to shine his light into this corner of her soul. She then *unburdened* her worries to Jesus as he drew near.

As a result of her Spirit-led self-leadership, Nicole gained confidence. The newly unburdened part of her soul was no longer fearful of losing God's love. Instead, it learned to courageously embrace the truth of his unconditional love. "I may not always care perfectly for everybody," she began telling herself. "But I'll do what I can and trust the rest to him."

Was Nicole selfish to say no from time to time? No. Did she have needs of her own? Very definitely.

Having released her burden of false guilt, Nicole was developing stronger internal boundaries and an identity of her own, rooted in her growing knowledge of God's love. And her guilt-tripping manager learned humility and reminded her to depend on God. Now she could joyfully build her own family life and incorporate her mom into it in ways that were healthy for everyone.

When your Spirit-led self is leading a part of your soul, that part will know and share what it needs to unburden. It doesn't matter *how* unburdening happens; what matters is that your burdens are gone. You may be surprised by the creative ways parts of your soul express themselves. For example, you may sense your shyness stepping out in courage or a fearful part becoming free. In the presence of God, these parts of your internal family will see and become the version of themselves they were created to be.

WHAT ARE BURDENS?

Burdens are the extreme beliefs, feelings, or even physical problems that parts of you take on as a result of painful experiences. You can develop burdens anytime, but they often develop in childhood. For example, when you were a young child, your mind couldn't process complex experiences. And so, at some point in the past, you interpreted events in ways that weren't helpful. Parts of your soul may still be holding on to these beliefs and feelings.

Consider examples of different kinds of burdens, each with a different origin:

Belief Burdens

- *Someone's hurting me, so I must have done something wrong.*
- *One of my parents had an affair, so I'm going to have an affair too.*

- *I must take care of others to earn their love and approval.*
- *Powerful people are bad and can't be trusted.*
- *I have to be responsible for everyone around me.*

Feeling Burdens
- disproportionate anger
- a vague sense of unhappiness
- distrust of authority figures
- fear of commitment
- false guilt
- chronic shame
- a feeling of worthlessness
- self-doubt

Physical Burdens
- persistent headache
- tightness in your shoulders
- a knot in your stomach
- tension in your jaw
- insomnia

(Note that some physical issues are burdens caused by trauma and others are not.)

Rationally, you may understand that you don't need to feel or think the way you do and that the hurts you suffered were not your fault. But a part of you tenaciously bears a burden anyway. You may still be angry, for example, even though you may have removed yourself from unhealthy family dynamics. Or you may cling to regret, the only way you know to cope with loss. Although these emotions may have helped you survive difficult situations, it's time to put a gentle boundary around them and free them to play a more constructive role in your internal family.

WHERE DO BURDENS COME FROM?

Think of a time when a dream was shattered into a thousand pieces like a mug on a hard kitchen floor. Maybe a relationship ended, or you struggled in school. Perhaps you were bullied, neglected, or a loved one passed away. You gave meanings to those experiences—meanings that may still weigh you down.

Burdens also come from disappointments that occur in the present. You might be struggling in your career. Perhaps you have a chronic illness, or your family life is not what you dreamed it would be. Maybe you feel betrayed by a friend. While your protectors are busy helping you cope, exiles often harbor unhelpful beliefs and feelings. Any challenging circumstance has the potential to affect a constellation of parts.

LEGACY BURDENS

You also can pick up burdens through your family or the culture in which you were raised. In his helpful book *The Body Keeps the Score*, trauma specialist Bessel van der Kolk wrote, "Traumatic experiences do leave traces, whether on a large scale (on our histories and cultures) or close to home, on our families, with dark secrets being imperceptibly passed down through generations."[1] Psychotherapist Richard Schwartz, founder of IFS, calls these traces "legacy burdens."[2] Our parents' unresolved burdens may impact our lives for decades, "to the third and fourth generation" (Ex. 34:7).

My, Kim's, paternal grandfather was a United States Marine who served in the battle of Iwo Jima during World War II. His duty was to defuse enemy bombs. He often had to come up with strategies to neutralize bombs on the spot. During this time, he faced the constant threat that the smallest mistake would cause the bombs to explode and kill both him and the men with whom he served.

So it's not surprising that, when his son, my father, earned a 98 percent on a test, my grandfather would focus on the 2 percent that were wrong. The hardworking part of my grandfather that fought for freedom remained disappointed with imperfection long after the war had ended. As a result of his war experience, he was focused on achieving perfection in all areas of his life.

My loyal grandfather's well-intended perfectionism had a big effect on my father, whose tender heart developed tenacious internal protectors. Once, after he had called to tell me about yet another breakup with a lovely girlfriend, I asked if he had ever considered going to counseling. I'll never forget his sarcastic reply: "You think I want to look at what I've swept under the rug all these years?" This stance toward pain cost him three marriages. It's no wonder I love the saying, "Life's too short to sweep the elephant under the rug."

My father and grandfather wanted the best for me. They passed down to me persistence, a passion for life, and a perfectionism that I call my "reformer part," which I have to remind myself to befriend. My countervailing spiritual discipline is to see how many seconds I can breathe without having a thought of how something can be improved. As a recovering perfectionist, I've begun to discover what Richard Rohr described in his book on personality types as the goal for someone with my predisposition—cheerful tranquility.[3]

No matter how hard your caregivers tried, by the time you reach adulthood, you'll have inherited at least a burden or two. A burdened part can be like a soldier who doesn't know that the war has ended. This unsung hero continues fighting valiantly, awaiting a new command. In the presence of your Spirit-led self, however, it will be relieved to lay down its burdens.

THE QUEST FOR REDEMPTION

As we've seen throughout this book, many people have parts stuck in the past, seeking to unburden pain. A part of Megan (chapters 2 and 3) still thought she wasn't good enough, even though she had gained success. A part of Lin (chapter 4) felt powerless as an adult because of having been bullied as a child. A part of Tom (chapter 6) still felt overlooked, even though he had become a successful businessman. Years had come and gone for each of these people, and they had moved on in many ways. But they all had parts that were stuck and holding on to painful memories.

Parts like these, stuck in the past, can lead you (or sometimes drag you!) into relationships where they hope to be redeemed, causing you to be hurt again and again. They self-sabotage by focusing attention on someone in your world who looks, talks, acts, and sounds similar to the person who originally wounded you. Their well-intended desire is to re-create childhood relationship dynamics in hopes of redeeming your past.[4] In doing so, however, they actually *create* the situation they're trying to avoid. The following persistent thoughts can signal the presence of an exile on a quest for redemption: *The man I like is just like my father; he will give me the affection I never received.* Or, *If I could just get her to love me, then I wouldn't feel so worthless.*

To further complicate matters, sometimes parts of us get mixed up about God too. Developmentally, young parts don't know the difference between people and God. Parents, caregivers, or even church leaders who represent God to young minds inevitably disappoint. As a result of human brokenness, young parts pick up beliefs that our adult selves may know to be untrue, such as: *God is a harsh taskmaster who is there to punish me; I have to be perfect to earn God's approval.*

You may know that these statements aren't true. Nevertheless, hurt and misinformed parts of your soul may carry these false beliefs. They keep you from receiving love and from loving God and others with your whole heart. We all have parts like these that need our loving attention. They need to invite Jesus to be near, unburden, and be updated about all Christ has to give.

THEN AND NOW

Unburdening means inviting an exile to move from the past into the present. You've moved forward, but this part carrying pain has not. Focus on the part that's alone and befriend it. Listen for the undercurrents of emotion or the beliefs the young part carries about its experiences, including misperceptions of God's role. As Henri Nouwen exhorted, "You have to bring home the part of you that was left behind."[5]

When your Spirit-led self connects with your exile, update it about all the strengths, resources, and wisdom you've gained over the years. Let it know there's more to who you are than it can see from its limited vantage point. Share the truth of who you are from God's perspective. Comforted by your attention, this tender exile can now release its burdensome feelings and misconceptions. Help this lost part of your soul join you in the present and integrate into your internal family where it can take comfort in your Spirit-led self and Jesus' love.

COMMON FEARS PROTECTORS HAVE ABOUT UNBURDENING

There's a reason we all say, "Change is hard!" A protector part you've befriended may not want to change its ways. This loyal part has worked for a long time to keep you from the painful feelings your exiles carry. Begin working with this protector by acknowledging

Ignoring Painful Emotions: Myth vs. Truth

Myth: Ignoring difficult emotions will make them go away.
Truth: Ignoring difficult emotions can send them to an isolated, untended place within your soul where they do not receive the care they need.

What helps is to befriend these parts of your soul and heal their painful memories. As parts that carry unwanted feelings sense the welcoming presence of your Spirit-led self, their intensity will soften, they will unburden, and they will take on new roles in your internal family. Your internal boundaries will grow healthy and strong.

the fears it carries regarding the inevitable change that unburdening an exile will bring. Here are some of the more common fears:[6]

The Fear of Being Overwhelmed

The pain will be overwhelming: *It's better not to go there!*

- **Response:** *I'm stronger than I think.* "When you pass through the waters, I will be with you; and when you pass through the rivers, they will not sweep over you. When you walk through the fire . . . the flames will not set you ablaze" (Isa. 43:2).

The Fear That It's Not Worth It

There's no benefit from revisiting the past: *What good will it do? What's the point? Nothing's ever going to change.*

- **Response:** *I'm going to face the past so that I can heal and move forward in new ways.* "See, I am doing a new thing!" (Isa. 43:19).

The Fear That It's Too Hard and Will Make Things Worse

Looking back will trigger dangerous firefighter behaviors: *I can't handle it!*

- **Response:** *Learning to tolerate difficult emotions is like developing a new muscle. It can be hard at first, but it makes me stronger and more capable.* "For I can do everything through Christ, who gives me strength" (Phil. 4:13 NLT).

Imagine That!

Honoring Valiant Protectors

In order to relax, your protectors may need to be honored for their years of hard work. My, Kim's, client Kate came to see me for her "anger problem." Once she connected with her loyal, angry protector in counseling, Kate discovered it was guarding her from the pain of an exile, shamed in her past. It was reluctant to let her exile unburden its pain, fearing it would no longer be needed or *important* to her. So, I suggested that she imagine a commemorative service to honor this valiant manager part that had protected her from being overwhelmed by her shame. Kate embraced this idea, and like a heroic war veteran, this protective, angry part came forward to receive its medal of honor for its years of faithful service. After this experience, Kate shared that she no longer wrestled with such strong feelings of anger.

The Fear of Loss of Identity

The part won't be needed anymore and, as a result, will lose its significance: *Everyone is used to me having this problem. Who will I be without it?*

• **Response**: *I am God's creation. This part of me will still have an important job to do.* "For we are God's masterpiece. He has created us anew in Christ Jesus, so we can do the good things he planned for us long ago" (Eph. 2:10 NLT).

If you've had any of these fears, they may be coming from your protectors. Before you unburden, assist them in facing their fears with curiosity and compassion. Protectors want to avoid shame at all costs. They want you to believe they're your best bet for staying safe and strong. Your protectors need to know that the Holy Spirit in you is more powerful than their habits and the outdated beliefs to which they've clung—they can let your Spirit-led self take the lead. They've worked hard to keep you from pain. What would it be like for these hardworking parts to find rest?

HOW TO UNBURDEN AN EXILE

Once a protector has given you permission to help an exile, connect with that vulnerable part of your soul from a place of curiosity and compassion. Now that you're leading from your Spirit-led self, it's safe to get closer to the painful thoughts and feelings your protector has worked so hard to keep far away. With an open heart, try to get to know this aspect of yourself better. Ask yourself, *What can I learn about this hurting part? Is it carrying any burdens—a feeling, a thought, an image, or a physical symptom?* Ask the part to tell you whatever it wants you to know. In the process, you'll be building stronger boundaries for your soul.

When you start paying attention to an exile, you may at first be flooded with emotion. At this point you might be tempted to give up, never completing the hard work of addressing your past. But the good news is that it's possible to connect with these parts of yourself and ask them to step back so your Spirit-led self can be of help. Richard Schwartz first discovered, and we can confirm from our work with clients, that once you're *present with* these vulnerable parts of your soul, you can ask them not to overwhelm you, and—relieved that you're taking the lead—they'll become calm.

COMMON FEARS EXILES HAVE ABOUT UNBURDENING

Even after an exile gains your trust and agrees not to overwhelm you, it still may have fears about unburdening painful beliefs and emotions. For example, the part may fear that your experience (and its hard work) will be forgotten. And as you saw in Nicole's story, exiles grow accustomed to being protected. As with your protectors, your exiles have played an important role in your life and can feel threatened by the idea of change. Common fears include:

The Fear That No One Will Remember All the Pain I've Experienced

If I forgive, it will be like the offense never happened. The person who offended me shouldn't get off the hook so easily.

- **Response:** *Though I may never forget, I can forgive. And God, who is perfectly just, remembers too.* "You keep track of all my sorrows. You have collected all my tears in your bottle. You have recorded each one in your book" (Ps. 56:8 NLT).

The Fear That I'm Not Worthy

I've failed in the past. Why should I expect anything else from myself now?

- **Response:** *I've learned from my mistakes. I'm not the same person anymore, and God is helping me grow day by day.* "We all, who with unveiled faces contemplate the Lord's glory, are being transformed into his image with ever-increasing glory" (2 Cor. 3:18).

The Fear of Abandonment

If I face this burden, someone will find out. Then, no one will ever want to be with me.

- **Response:** *People who love me will accept me with my flaws, and God's presence brings healing.* He says, "I will never fail you. I will never abandon you" (Heb. 13:5 NLT).

The Fear of Becoming Well

I don't know how to be well—that's just not me.

- **Response:** *I can embrace Jesus' invitation to heal and grow.* "When Jesus saw him lying there and learned that he had been in this condition for a long time, he asked him, 'Do you want to get well?'" (John 5:6).

The Fear That My Memory of a Loved One Will Fade

If I move forward with my own hopes and dreams, my loved one might be forgotten.

- **Response:** *I can create a space in my heart for this grief and still live my life. I can create rituals to remember the one that I love and move forward.* "All the days ordained for me were written in your book before one of them came to be" (Ps. 139:16).

ARE YOU READY TO EXCHANGE A BURDEN FOR A KNAPSACK?

The Bible teaches that each of us is meant to carry our own "knapsack" of problems, but shouldering heavy "boulders" is a call for action.[7] Are you carrying around painful feelings, such as guilt, bitterness, and fear? If so, how would you like to lay them down?

Think of a feeling burden as being carried by a weary part. Ask this part what it needs, and it will tell you. Using your imagination, unburdening can happen through reenvisioning a situation or through rescripting a belief or a narrative you've created. The process will be different each time you unburden a part. Using the God-given power of imagination, our clients unburden painful beliefs, feelings, and memories in these ways:

- They contain their shame in a bottle and toss it to God.
  - "Cast all your anxiety on him because he cares for you" (1 Peter 5:7).
- They shed their past hurt like a layer of clothing.
  - "You were taught, with regard to your former way of life, to put off your old self, which is being corrupted by its deceitful desires; to be made new in the attitude of your minds; and to put on the new self, created to be like God in true righteousness and holiness" (Eph. 4:22–24).
- They are purified of their burdens by a refining fire.
  - "He will sit like a refiner of silver, burning away the dross" (Mal. 3:3 NLT).
- They release them to be washed away by rain.
  - "As surely as the sun rises, he will appear; he will come to us like the winter rains, like the spring rains that water the earth" (Hos. 6:3).

- They send their guilt into the wounds of Christ.
  - "By his wounds we are healed" (Isa. 53:5).
- They draw near to the cross, receive new life, and find freedom from discouragement and despair.
  - "I want to know Christ and experience the mighty power that raised him from the dead. I want to suffer with him, sharing in his death, so that one way or another I will experience the resurrection from the dead!" (Phil. 3:10–11 NLT).

GET OUT OF THE VICTIM PLACE AND ASK FOR WHAT YOU WANT

Once a newly liberated exile has unburdened, make sure it has shaken off its passive rescue wishes.[8] It must learn to get out of the victim place and kindly ask for what it wants. When you experience the freedom that comes from being unburdened, ask God for strengths and resources to help you thrive. What gift would you like to receive from God in order to be made whole?

You might choose one of the fruits of the Holy Spirit: love, joy, peace, patience, kindness, goodness, faithfulness, gentleness, and self-control (Gal. 5:22–23 NLT). You may want to help this part of yourself acclimate to God's loving presence, taking in what it feels like to be near him. Or, as described by the IFS approach, you may become, for example, calm, caring, confident, creative, courageous, and clear.[9] Check in with the part you've helped unburden; parts always know what they need.

You'll discover that their new qualities will help you become your best self and fulfill your God-given potential. Their capacity for engaging with others and contemplating beauty will awaken in you a new sense of wonder. Unburdening does not mean you won't feel a full range of emotions, including sadness and anger.

Suffer what you have to suffer, but don't suffer what you don't have to suffer.

Remember, however: *Suffer what you have to suffer, but don't suffer what you don't have to suffer.* Even though your circumstances may not change, you can experience more joy when you release your burdens to God.

RENAMING

When a part unburdens and takes on new qualities, you may want to give it a new name. The Bible says, "No longer will they call you Deserted, or name your land Desolate . . . for the LORD will take delight in you" (Isa. 62:4). God will "bestow on [you] a crown of beauty instead of ashes, the oil of joy instead of mourning, and a garment of praise instead of a spirit of despair" (61:3). Once a part of your soul unburdens, ask yourself: *What new name makes sense now?* As you do this work of drawing new boundary lines and renaming aspects of your internal family, you participate in expanding God's reign—within your internal terrain.

If a part of you is carrying a burden, it needs your Spirit-led self to show up for it and, in a posture of prayer, invite Jesus to draw near. Richard Schwartz authored a book titled *You Are the One You've Been Waiting For.* And we would add that God, working through your Spirit-led self, is the ultimate source of all you need.

UNBURDENING A PART OF YOURSELF

When you've experienced trauma or loss, what stories have you told yourself? Are you ready to trade a myth for a truthful new narrative? What burdens have outstayed their welcome in your soul? This exercise will help you gain perspective and unburden painful feelings and beliefs. As you undertake this step in particular, you may want to find a trusted friend, mentor, spiritual director, or professional counselor to journey with you.

Think of a recent situation that evokes a strong emotion in you. For example, are you feeling stressed at work or weary of your responsibilities at home? Is a part of you struggling with sorrow or feeling unloved? Can you describe that feeling?

Examples:

I feel lonely.
I feel ashamed.
I feel afraid.

Now let the circumstance that led to the feeling fade away, and focus your attention on the feeling itself.

Ask yourself, *How do I feel toward the part of myself feeling this way?*

Examples:

I'm mad at myself for feeling this way.
I feel guilty about this feeling.
I'm afraid it will never go away.

If you recognize anything but curiosity and compassion, then you've identified another part of yourself. See if this part will give you some space to allow you to focus on your original feeling.

Return to that original part with curiosity, and see how present you can be with this part of your soul without being overwhelmed by it. Once you've connected with this part, extend it your compassion, as you would extend compassion to a friend. Then ask:

- What is an extreme belief or feeling that burdens this part?

Examples:
- ○ *I'm unimportant.*
- ○ *If I could just get someone to love me, then I wouldn't feel so alone.*
- ○ *If I could be perfect, she would finally pay attention to me.*
- Does this part have any fears about giving up those burdens? (You may want to refer to the fears of exiles, listed earlier in this chapter.)
- How does this part want to give those burdens to God? (Refer to the list of ways to unburden earlier in this chapter, or see if the part has its own idea.)
- What gift might God have for this part of you in return?

The good news is this: *Your burdens have a place to go.* Hurting parts of your soul can release the weight they've been carrying. God invites you to get away with him. And when God joins you in your pain, he "won't lay anything heavy or ill-fitting on you. Keep company with [him] and you'll learn to live freely and lightly" (Matt. 11:28–30 MSG).

Through the process of unburdening, you can create more spaciousness in your soul for your Spirit-led self. From this place, unburdened parts can join you in pursuing a purposeful life of service and love for others. Howard Thurman (1889–1981), mentor to Martin Luther King Jr., once said that when there is reconciliation, "the wildness is gentled out of a personality at war with itself."[10]

The ministry of reconciliation to which we are called (2 Cor. 5:18) includes reconciliation *within*. Would you now like to negotiate internal reconciliation—an ingathering among the many diverse, competing aspects of yourself—and create a powerful team of rivals? Would you like to put the unburdened parts of your soul to work for God's kingdom? If so, turn to the next chapter to discover how.

Chapter 8

STEP FIVE: INTEGRATE

Keep your friends close and your enemies closer.
—MICHAEL CORLEONE, *THE GODFATHER PART II*

*Jesus knew their thoughts and said to them: "Any
kingdom divided against itself will be ruined,
and a house divided against itself will fall."*
—LUKE 11:17

How DO YOU turn your internal rivals into a team that works together? When you take a You-Turn, you *focus, befriend, invite,* and *unburden* parts of yourself in need, one at a time. Now, in step 5, you *integrate* those parts into your internal family. Parts that were at odds take on new roles. It can be helpful to look for other examples of people who have turned rivals into friends and recruited them to be on their team. Perhaps the best example is President Abraham Lincoln.

PRESIDENT LINCOLN'S TEAM OF RIVALS

On June 16, 1858, on the steps of the Illinois State Capitol, Abraham Lincoln spoke to a nation deeply divided over slavery:

A house divided against itself cannot stand. I believe this government cannot endure, permanently, half slave and half free. I do not expect the Union to be dissolved—I do not expect the house to fall—but I do expect it will cease to be divided.[1]

At the time he delivered his "House Divided" speech, Lincoln was still a prairie lawyer whose highest elected position was one term in the House of Representatives, but he was gaining attention as an eloquent critic of slavery. Within two years, he would make a long-shot bid for the presidency. Standing in his way were several of the nation's leading political figures—men who were better known, more experienced, and, on paper, better suited for the high office. Each of these men believed that he, not Lincoln, should be president. In a surprise victory, however, Lincoln defeated his rivals and won the election of 1860. As soon as the votes were counted, the new president-elect was immediately thrust into the deepest crisis in the nation's history. Before he could even take the oath of office, seven states seceded from the Union, and the nation was on a path to civil war. The "divided house" was about to fall.

Lincoln knew he needed a team of the nation's best leaders to confront this crisis. He turned to several of the prominent men who had been his rivals—men he had defeated for the presidency—and invited them into his inner circle, the cabinet. He asked one to be his secretary of state, another his secretary of the treasury, a third his attorney general, and a fourth his secretary of war. Although it was a challenge to do so, he knew that he needed to turn these capable "enemies" into his allies and advisers. As Doris Kearns Goodwin highlighted in her bestselling Lincoln biography, *Team of Rivals*, Lincoln displayed political genius by recognizing the value of making friends with his opponents.[2]

In time these former rivals served Lincoln with devotion and distinction to hold together the nation as it was being split in two. Although the Civil War was a bitter struggle, in the end Lincoln sought a restored nation through reconciliation and friendship with the other side. "With malice toward none," he urged, "with charity for all . . . [let us] do all which may achieve and cherish a just and lasting peace among ourselves and with all nations."[3]

Lincoln's idea of the "house divided" had been inspired by the words of Jesus in the gospel of Luke: "Any kingdom divided against itself will be ruined, and a house divided against itself will fall" (11:17). Although Jesus was speaking of the spiritual realm, Lincoln applied the principle to the nation. In a similar way, you can let Jesus' warning about a house divided inspire you to have an undivided heart and to turn your internal enemies into your greatest allies.

RESOLVING POLARIZATIONS

The North and the South were polarized before the Civil War. And sometimes you might feel that parts of your soul are engaged in a similar struggle. An internal polarization is "a state in which two members (or groups) . . . relate in opposition to or in competition with each other, to the point where each party's access to the Self is constrained by fear that the other party will win or take over."[4] This dynamic leads to division and conflicts within your soul. Reconciliation, on the other hand, resolves conflict between you and God, you and others, and also within yourself. The Bible encourages the "ministry of reconciliation" (2 Cor. 5:17–20). Applied internally, reconciliation involves setting boundaries and restoring peace among the adversarial members of your internal family.

How do you know when you have a polarization in your soul? When your Spirit-led self tries to befriend a part of yourself and another part gets in the way, you might have two polarized parts. This dynamic occurs between protectors. For example, you might have an internal people-pleaser working hard to keep the peace while an inner critic seizes every opportunity to notice others' flaws. Your people-pleaser, terrified that your critic might hurt someone and embarrass you in the process, works overtime to keep everyone in your life happy. Meanwhile, your critic, resentful of any attempt at restraint, doubles down and becomes even more negative. Both parts are trying valiantly to keep your exiles from getting hurt; however, their strategies are polar opposites.

When you discover a polarization, work with both parts and then negotiate between them. Starting with the part that's most present to you, focus on it, befriend it, and learn its perspective. Assure it of its value too. What are its fears and concerns about modifying its role? Invite Jesus to be near it. Then see if this part would be willing to step back and watch quietly as you work with the second part. If so, repeat the process with the second part. (If not, continue working compassionately and patiently with the first part until it's able to cooperate.) As you connect with these conflicting dimensions of your soul from your Spirit-led self, explore how they can learn from each other and work together to achieve their common goal: helping your internal family thrive. Let's see how one client accomplished this mission.

Imagine That!

RUBEN'S STORY: NEGOTIATING A PEACE TREATY

"The dating world is tough!" Ruben said to me, Kim, in session. "For years I've tried to walk the straight and narrow, but sometimes I want to throw caution to the wind!"

Ruben was having trouble developing a meaningful relationship. He had a moralistic manager part that kept him from getting into trouble. But because this side of him was so domineering, he had developed a polarized part that couldn't help but flirt with his female friends and coworkers. Ruben's critical internal manager berated his flirting firefighter part, creating anxiety inside whenever he had a chance to get close to women. As you can imagine, this approach wasn't bringing Ruben success in the dating arena.

I asked Ruben to focus on how he was feeling and let me know if he could imagine the part that wanted to be good and moral. He said he could imagine himself at a younger age wearing a T-shirt that said "Off Limits" in bright yellow letters. This internal protector part didn't want to be seen as a player and would try to keep him from ever expressing interest in women.

After we let Ruben's off-limits part share for a bit, I asked how he felt toward it. He said he hated it because it was annoying and kept him from having any fun. This annoyed part wouldn't step back when we asked it to do so, however, so we realized that Ruben had an internal polarization. I asked Ruben if he could imagine the part that didn't like his strict part. He said yes, he saw an image of himself wearing his cool leather jacket, hanging out in a bar. I asked what he wanted to name this part. "Flirting with temptation," he said. This side of Ruben liked to walk too close to the line and crossed it every now and then. For example, once he had initiated a one-night stand, much to the chagrin of his moralistic manager.

Now that Ruben had befriended both his sanctimonious, off-limits part and his straying, flirting-with-temptation part, it was time to see if they would be willing to work together. To start the process of negotiating between these two rivals, I asked Ruben which one needed his attention first. Ruben decided to start with "flirting with temptation."

I knew that Ruben loved Jesus and desired to follow him, so I asked, "Would your flirting-with-temptation part like to invite Jesus to be near?"

"Yes," he replied. And soon he was able to sense Jesus' loving presence there with him. Ruben was surprised to find that Jesus welcomed his straying firefighter and didn't judge it. With Jesus near, and in the presence of his Spirit-led self, this newly "boundaried" part showed Ruben that it didn't really want to have one-night stands; it just wanted a little more freedom to enjoy dating. As a tribute to its remarkable transformation, Ruben decided to rename this loyal protector his "enjoying life" part. Feeling honored, it then gave Ruben permission to return his attention to the off-limits part to see if it was aware of what had just occurred.

Indeed, this part had seen that Jesus understood his flirting-with-temptation part and its desire to enjoy life. Now his off-limits part became aware of feeling tired. And it no longer had a job to do, given that his Spirit-led self was now in charge. So Ruben prayerfully imagined giving it a medal of honor for its years of faithful service working to keep him out of trouble. He sensed it was happy to receive the medal. It then needed a new role, one that was still important but not as strident. When Ruben checked to see what new role this hardworking aspect of his soul wanted, in his mind's eye, he saw his off-limits part change its T-shirt and put on one that said, "Proceed with caution."

As Ruben invited Jesus to draw near this newly boundaried moralistic manager, the first thing Jesus did was compliment the off-limits part about its medal. Then the part handed its old T-shirt to Jesus.

Through the power of prayerful imagination, Ruben envisioned both his proceed-with-caution part and his enjoying-life part sitting around a table. Both had found that they could learn from one another and that their agendas weren't mutually exclusive. As a result, they were excited for Ruben to start dating in a healthy way, and they thanked God together.

Creating internal boundaries requires negotiating with competing parts of your soul, to unite them around your values, commitments, and goals. The opposing factions within your soul won't work together without your Spirit-led self to guide them to compromise. Prayerfully ministering to hurting aspects of yourself helps build your own team of rivals and transform them into cooperative members of your internal family. You'll be surprised how readily they're willing to cooperate once they realize they're on the same team. As he matured, King David experienced this internal cohesion when he prayed: "I will praise you, Lord my God, with my whole heart" (Ps. 86:12 WEB).

The framers of the U.S. Constitution envisioned a diversity of interests arguing their way to a common goal. We're all at our best when engaged in vigorous debate. As a society and as individuals, we flourish when we have confidence in our arguments *and* the courage to listen to our opponents, giving them the benefit of the doubt. And the same is true of the many aspects of your soul. Don't stop listening to the people—or to the parts of yourself—who disagree with you. Put yourself in their shoes and seek to understand their perspective. You won't like everything they say, but you'll make better decisions if you hear them out.

ASSIGNING NEW ROLES

Once reconciled, competing parts will feel relieved to take on new roles. When you've *focused*, *befriended*, *invited*, and *unburdened* them, update them on your life's achievements and all the things you would still like to accomplish. Then ask them what different, more helpful strategies they can adopt to accomplish their goal of helping you. Ask them what new roles they would like to play. This process of *integration* leads to a lighter way of being. You might notice the following "holy reframes" in your thinking:

- "I can't take the pain" becomes "I am stronger than I think."

- "I'm not important" becomes "It matters that I'm here."
- "I'll never be as good as other people" becomes "No one can take my place."
- "No one loves me" becomes "I am God's beloved child."
- "My life has no purpose" becomes "How can I serve today?"

How has practicing Spirit-led self-leadership helped each person mentioned in this book develop an internal team of rivals?

In chapters 2 and 3, we met Megan, who had a striving task manager that wouldn't let her rest. Eventually, this hardworking part softened and learned to trust in the leadership of Megan's Spirit-led self. Her task manager became a skilled adviser, taking into account her need to rest and play.

In chapter 4 we met Lin, a pediatric resident, who was angry at everyone around her. Guided by the gentleness of her Spirit-led self, Lin's anger became her adviser. She learned to detect unsafe people—or rather, people with unsafe parts. Instead of waiting for others to change, she became more proactive in cultivating healthy boundaries.

In chapter 5, we met Margaret, who had been cutting herself to numb painful emotions. Margaret's well-intended cutting part became her advocate once her Spirit-led self took the lead. It learned to champion—not numb—her tenderness by speaking out on her behalf when others were hurting her. And her tender exile, now closer to her Spirit-led self, revealed a gentleness that surprised and delighted those who earned her trust.

In chapter 6 we met Tom, whose pride was on the verge of ruining his marriage. Tom's pride, once it gave him some space, became his humble confidence as he brought it into harmony with the part of himself that had been feeling insignificant. The warring parts of Tom's soul were now on board with a new mission: to regain his family's trust and to be a loving husband and father. Instead of overcompensating for his feelings of unworthiness, he learned to value the vulnerable parts of his soul and speak kindly to his wife and kids.

In chapter 7 we met Nicole, who felt overwhelmed with guilt whenever she set a healthy boundary with her mom. Nicole learned the difference between caring for others out of fear and caring for others with God-given humility. Once contained within healthy boundaries, her guilt-tripper transformed into a part that reminded her to depend on God. Unburdening her false guilt resulted in a newfound courage to advocate for her own needs.

And in this chapter, we met Ruben, who was torn between viewing dating as "off limits" and "flirting with temptation." Ruben finally learned how to treat a woman with respect and have fun dating too. His flirting-with-temptation part felt understood by Jesus and no longer wanted to cross moral lines. Instead, it taught him to kick up his heels and show a girl a good time—while maintaining good boundaries. And his moral, off-limits part learned to trust that his desire to date was healthy and fun. As a result, it relaxed and helped him to communicate clearly with women about his intentions.

What would it be like if *your* warring parts worked together in this way—if your managers, firefighters, and exiles adopted more helpful roles and became, to paraphrase Lincoln, the better angels of your nature?[5] What if a controlling part of you became a loving coach, led by your Spirit-led self? What energy have you spent "firefighting" that now could be channeled into achieving your life's mission? Likewise, what exile within you wants to encourage someone else in pain? As different aspects of your soul shed their old ways, you'll be able to harness their energy into a powerful team of (former) rivals. You might be surprised at what roles your fiercest protectors and most timid exiles would like to have when invited to dream. As Helen LaKelly Hunt wisely wrote:

The Seven Deadly Sins can become aspects of a healthy self. Greed and lust become passion, imbuing our journey with heart and fire. Anger transforms into righteousness that acts compassionately for our own and others' behalf. The healthy side to gluttony is self-care, something many [people] have to learn. Envy, once integrated, becomes an appreciation of others. And in a society where doing is valued over being, sloth turns into the ability to be still. Pride enables us to feel good about our accomplishments and grow in confidence and strength.[6]

THE GATHERING IN YOUR SOUL

In the Sermon on the Mount, Jesus invited the strong to humble themselves, and at the same time, he described as blessed those who are poor, hungry, hurting, and sick (Matt. 5:1–12; 6:5). The same paradoxical truths apply within your soul. Imagine your strong protectors and vulnerable exiles sitting together around a table, each part sharing in the goodness of God's presence—none complete without the other. Remember the words of Jesus: when you hold a feast, invite the poor, the crippled, the lame, the blind, and you will be blessed (Luke 14:13–14). Jesus invites all people to come to him. Another way of looking at this verse is that he invites *every part of you* to come to him as well. All parts of you are welcome, no matter how broken or rejected they may feel.

BECOMING WHOLE

I, Alison, experience a glimpse of Jesus' vision of integration at our church, held in a homeless shelter operated by the Salvation Army. A diverse representation of God's kingdom attends our weekly Bible study, each one bringing a different gift—and struggle—to the gathering. Around our circle sit several women next to grocery bags holding all of their possessions, former prisoners fighting addiction, and faithful elderly women who have turned their grief over losing family members into encouragement of those in recovery. My husband and I complete the circle, our tragedies and hardships perhaps not as obvious to the group but no less present.

On one of our first nights leading the group, a woman joined us who suffered from mental illness. Every few minutes, she would interrupt to share details about her extensive collection of orange peels. Feeling anxious, I quickly left the room to ask my pastor for advice about how to help her stay focused. My pastor kindly replied, "I'd try to get to know her just as she is." I returned to the group realizing that my anxious task manager had eclipsed my Spirit-led self, and I had almost missed an opportunity to welcome the woman as Jesus would. As we continued, I noticed how attentively everyone listened to her, even though it was nearly impossible to understand what she was saying. Her face began to shine, and her urgent need to share started to wane. Afterward, she thanked the group several times for including her, promising to bring us a few of her beloved orange peels the next time we met. Experiencing the warmth of her kindness and the generous nature of her spirit was far more important to our spiritual growth that night than my carefully planned Bible study.

In our weekly gatherings, I have caught a glimpse of what Jesus meant when he turned the tables on the notion of the strong and the weak—when we all come together, there is tremendous spiritual power. And the same truth applies to the parts of your soul: What might happen inside of you as you gather your strong protectors and vulnerable exiles and listen attentively to each one? You might be surprised as your protectors gain humble perspective and your exiles shine more light than you ever thought possible. The more you integrate your strengths and vulnerabilities, the more whole you become.

RESTORING HARMONY

The human soul, when carefully tended, is like a beautiful garden. This striking similarity has helped as I, Kim, have learned the importance of backyard biodiversity and cultivating an ecosystem in which plants help one another thrive. In my garden, native plants such as yarrow, lilac, and rosemary cross-pollinate. Monarch butterflies thrive near sagebrush and seaside daisies. Redwood trees planted in clusters strengthen one another when their roots intermingle underground.

So it is with the ecology of your soul. When you practice Spirit-led self-leadership, you're cultivating an internal garden that helps the wild and magnificent parts of you grow together in a peaceful and integrated way. Each part becoming healthier generates growth in other areas of your internal landscape too.

If you garden you already know: You don't tend an entire garden all at once. Instead, you focus your attention on one aspect after another. You know that growth cannot be forced or rushed. The same is true with Spirit-led self-leadership. As you focus on dimensions of your soul in need of care one by one, gradually you'll see the beauty of blossoms and fruit that God brings forth. Whether cultivating a garden in your yard or an abundant inner landscape, you can say with the psalmist, "He makes me lie down in green pastures; He leads me beside quiet waters. He restores my soul" (Ps. 23:2–3 NASB).

A HOUSE UNITED

God designed you to have different feelings simultaneously. When you're broken, you experience conflict and chaos. In the integrated self, all parts of you are on the same team and exist in harmony.

Reconciling your inner world involves restoring Spirit-led harmony. Becoming healthy involves negotiating between conflicting feelings and getting them on board with a common mission.

As your protectors soften and gain more perspective and your exiles are brought into the love of your internal family, your house becomes unified and your mission becomes clear. Following the creative movements of the Spirit, you discover the motivation to pour yourself out for others. As Frederick Buechner so eloquently wrote, you find that place where your "deep gladness and the world's deep hunger meet."[7]

When you practice Spirit-led self-leadership, you're cultivating an internal garden that helps the wild and magnificent parts of you grow together in a peaceful and integrated way.

Delineating your own internal boundaries empowers you to care well for others. Your contemplative dwelling place motivates courageous and faithful service. Gaining a greater sense of internal order, you become free to focus on your God-given purpose in the world. You love people in a more merciful and sustainable way.

HELD TOGETHER IN ALL CIRCUMSTANCES

Whatever your challenges, when you learn to integrate your internal team of rivals, your service to others will lead to a life of deep peace. Again, looking to the apostle Paul, a servant who poured himself out for others, we find an example of an integrated soul. Toward the end of his life, he wrote even while sitting chained up in a jail cell, "I have learned the secret of being content in any and every situation" (Phil. 4:12). The English word *content* comes from the Latin word *contentus*, combining the words *held* and *together*. Being content implies an experience of being held together, contained, and well ordered internally, regardless of your external circumstances.

There's no need to hide from challenging aspects of yourself; establish gentle boundaries with them and lead them from your Spirit-led self. I, Alison, can now lead my empowered dreamer part to help others mend and reshape their broken dreams. And I still have to remind my smile-and-nod protector to practice listening to what's really going on in my soul *before* offering well-intended but sometimes premature assurances that "everything's fine."

I, Kim, can now lead my reformer part to help others be still in the presence of God—to connect with their deepest desires and discern God's calling for their lives. Yet this reformer part of me still needs to practice "just being" in my garden, a place where I learn and grow. And I still have to remind my sad part at times that I am loved by my Father in heaven and by my wonderful family and friends. We are all of these parts; we are wounded and we are becoming whole.

Change may take time, but our hope is that you'll be motivated to pursue the lost sheep within your soul and welcome them home. Participate in God's work of giving you "an undivided heart" (Ezek. 11:19). Then your character shines; you're the same person whether people are looking or not. Through the power of the Holy Spirit, you're held together in your innermost being. And you take on life's trials and the work God has given you to do with confidence and grace.

A TOWN-HALL MEETING EXERCISE

Imagine two parts of yourself that you're most aware of right now taking turns at the microphone at a town-hall meeting.[8]

1. What's the strongest feeling that you're having?

    Example: A cautious part of Ruben felt strongly that it's important to be careful when interacting with women.

2. Is there another part of you that doesn't like that you feel this way?

    Example: The risk-taking part of Ruben didn't like his cautious part.

3. What does this second part want the first part to know?

    Example: It wanted Ruben to know that it's important to take appropriate risks and enjoy life.

4. In response, what does the first part that spoke want this second part to know?

    Example: Ruben's cautious part wanted his risk-taking part to be guided by moral boundaries.

5. Prayerfully consider: What does Jesus want to say to both parts of you?

When both parts of you have been heard, identify their common goals and negotiate new strategies for working together. Are they aware of each other's good intentions and are they willing to work together? When the competing parts of your soul are willing to get behind the same mission, well done; your (former) rivals are becoming a team.

Part III

WORKING WITH CHALLENGING EMOTIONS

In PARTS I and II, we explored how to transform the challenging parts of your soul from enemies into allies. In this third section, we look more closely at how this process works when addressing specific emotions. We demonstrate how taking a You-Turn can help you find comfortable distance from—and a positive relationship with—parts with strong feelings. As you lead them from your Spirit-led self, the parts of your soul carrying anger, fear, sadness, envy, and shame can find much-needed rest and become your most loyal aides and advisers.

Explore throughout these pages what it would be like to live with healthy internal boundaries and an undivided heart. There's no need to read the next chapters sequentially. Each chapter stands alone and provides a path to follow when you're struggling (or helping someone else who's struggling) with the specific emotion being addressed. And if you notice yourself struggling with one of these emotions, work through the Five Steps located in the exercise at the back of the book. We've seen this Spirit-led approach bring healing and joy to many lives, and we know God has wonderful things in store for you.

Chapter 9

BOUNDARIES WITH ANGER

If we do not transform our pain, we
will most assuredly transmit it.

—Richard Rohr

Go ahead and be angry. You do well to be angry—
but don't use your anger as fuel for revenge. And
don't stay angry. Don't go to bed angry. Don't give
the Devil that kind of foothold in your life.

—Ephesians 4:26 (msg)

an·ger

ˈaNGgər/

noun

"a strong feeling of annoyance, displeasure, or hostility"[1]

Someone hurts you . . . maybe once, maybe twice, maybe many times, and the most natural response is to feel anger. A part of you may even want to punish the person who hurt you. Anger feels empowering in the moment but leads to feelings of guilt, sadness, and even shame. If you don't address your anger, before long you'll feel chaotic inside.

BOUNDARIES FOR YOUR SOUL

The prophet Jonah was no stranger to anger. He was angry at God for showing compassion toward the Ninevites, even after they had repented of their rebellion. He told God, "I'm so angry I wish I were dead" (Jonah 4:1–9). Jonah's bitterness prompted him to run away from God and almost lose his life. And it nearly prevented the good news of God's gracious forgiveness from reaching thousands of people.

Many of us have parts of our souls that get angry like Jonah. Bitterness takes root in our souls, and we end up wishing harm on those who have hurt us, instead of desiring for them to receive God's forgiveness. If you've had this experience, you know the damage anger can cause in your life.

In general, where are you in relation to your anger? Put a mark on the graph below to indicate your answer:

Too Close————Comfortable Distance————Too Far

GABE TAKES A YOU-TURN WHEN HE FEELS ANGER

A clenched fist. That's what came to his mind when I, Kim, asked Gabe to describe his anger. His wife had given him an ultimatum: "Get some counseling for your problem or leave the house," and he didn't want to leave her and their baby daughter.

As we began our first counseling session, Gabe didn't seem like an angry person, slouching on the couch in my office, gently running his fingers over the callouses on his weathered hands. His demeanor was soft-spoken and kind. His boots showed wear and tear from his work in construction.

"I have a hot temper," Gabe confided when I asked what brought him in. "I'm the one with the issue," he admitted, signaling his readiness to take a You-Turn.

"What happens when your temper flares up?" I asked.

"I yell at my wife," he said softly. "And not just at her—last week I threw her brother out of the house. He was trashing a ball-player. I'd had a long day, and I let loose on him. And then I crashed and slept too late the next day. I don't know why I did that. I don't know how to be the kind of husband my wife needs . . . the kind of father my daughter deserves."

As Gabe described his dilemma, I imagined a dashboard with one switch. Adrenaline flipped it on; depression flipped it off. Gabe's emotions were polarized. He was either hot-tempered or numb.

Focus

"Have you thought of listening to your anger?" I asked Gabe. And right then, in our first session, he closed his eyes and told me he saw a clenched fist. "It wants to punch everyone," he said, describing what he saw and heard. "It doesn't think I stand up for myself."

As Gabe focused on his anger, he began to reminisce about growing up with his drug-addicted father. He shared what it was like when a gang broke into his family home and beat up his dad in front of his impressionable, seven-year-old eyes. No one had been there to help this young boy understand his emotions and relate to them constructively. As a result, for years an angry part of his soul remained enraged and helpless at the same time.

When I asked what he wanted to say to his anger, Gabe took a moment in prayer and replied calmly, "That everything's okay now." Then, in the presence of his Spirit-led self, he imagined the clenched fist opening up, as if to say it was now ready to receive freely from God. After years of clenching his fist, Gabe was learning how to be openhanded.

"I feel peace. I want more of that," Gabe said, and so we set a time to meet again.

At our second session, Gabe confessed that he had, once again, been short-tempered with his wife: "At dinner she told me that she needed more grocery money. Then she reminded me to pick our daughter up at her mother's. I told her to get off my back . . . and that I take enough 'stuff' all day long," he said, not wanting to repeat the expletive to his Christian counselor. He explained that he was surrounded by men at work who often made a game of trying to make him watch pornography and violent videos. Even though he stood his ground, he would leave work angry and take his frustration out on his wife. This time Gabe said he saw his anger as a ball of fire—furious about what was happening at work.

Befriend

"How do you feel toward your angry part that looks like a ball of fire?" I asked.

Gabe said he felt critical of it. At my suggestion, he asked this disapproving part to step aside so we could get to know his anger better. And it did.

Now, as Gabe listened with curiosity to this part, he was surprised at what it said: "Fight for your family! Stop cursing at the guys at work! You can do better than that!"

He realized that his anger wasn't mad at other people—it wanted *him* to be better. This part of Gabe actually cared a lot about him and his family. And now it was beginning to see that swearing and yelling was getting him nowhere.

As Gabe connected to his anger from his Spirit-led self, he visibly began to relax. *Befriending* his anger and setting a gentle boundary around it was helping it settle down. "Now it looks like a candle with a peaceful glow," he said.

Invite

"Is Jesus near?" I asked, wondering if this fiery part of Gabe had a sense of God's presence.

Without hesitation he said, "Yes. Jesus is saying, 'No matter what darkness you face, the light will shine because I am the light.'

"He's also assuring me that he'll never leave me," Gabe concluded peacefully.

We checked in with the disapproving part of Gabe and found it was no longer critical. It wanted to be close to Jesus too. "Should we still call it 'the disapproving part,'" I asked, "or does it want a different name?"

Continuing in this state of listening prayer, Gabe replied, "Let's call it my overcomer. It doesn't want to be distrustful anymore. Jesus is saying to it, 'Nothing is impossible with me.'"

Through his prayerful imagination, Gabe practiced listening to God's voice and invited Jesus to draw near the angry part of his soul. As a result, his disapproving part wanted to be near Jesus too.

Unburden

As we approached the end of our session together, I asked Gabe whether he wanted to get rid of any burdens. Together we identified that the burden his anger carried was his extreme belief that the best way to deal with his pain was to yell. And he was tired of fighting his way through life. I asked how he wanted to unburden this belief, and he said he wanted to open his hands before Jesus and surrender his anger to him.

"I feel calmer," Gabe said after unburdening. "And now when I feel anger, I can open my hands and ask for help."

"Do you need anything else from Jesus?" I asked.

"Just for him to stay with me," Gabe replied. "I can sense him saying, 'I'll always be there to help you.'"

After this experience, I asked Gabe, "What stood out to you?"

"How easy it is to hear Jesus," he earnestly replied. "And how Jesus assured me that he is always there."

Summary of Gabe's You-Turn

Taking a You-Turn was helping Gabe to become the kind of man he wanted to be. Gabe grew to speak more kindly with his wife—*on behalf of* his anger, instead of *from* it. And he became more playful and present with their daughter too.

Gabe's experience of befriending anger helped heal the memory of his dad's beating. Now, when Gabe feels inclined to clench his fist, he stops to connect with this angry part of himself. Pausing gives him the space he needs to come up with a more constructive strategy than yelling at others or shutting down. Throughout the day, when he notices his anger, he reminds himself that he doesn't have to react in the moment. Gabe is learning to be neither passive nor aggressive, but to be assertive in a healthy way.

GETTING TO KNOW ANGER

"He has an anger problem!" Have you ever heard someone say that? Or how about, "She's such an angry person!" Or maybe even, "Oh no! I think I'm the one with the anger problem!" Once, after working with her anger, a client confessed to me, Kim, that she had been afraid to let me know how angry she really was at her ex-husband, because she was afraid that I would report her to the police. The way our anger overtakes us can be frightening.

Still, it doesn't help to think of yourself, or anyone else, as an "angry person." In fact, labeling invalidates other characteristics of a person and causes anger to dig in its heels in stubborn defiance. Instead, see your anger as one part of yourself among many other parts, and approach it with curiosity and compassion. Without a doubt, it is there for a good reason and has something valuable to offer.

Without internal boundaries, your anger can burn like a destructive fire. Contained within healthy boundaries, however, anger motivates you to be an agent of change. Developing comfortable distance with your anger involves appreciating its perspective and understanding what it's protecting.

Typically, anger protects a more vulnerable emotion exiled underneath it. So when you feel angry, take a You-Turn to put your anger to work for you: *Befriend* it by appreciating its good intentions and discovering what hurting exile within you it's been protecting. Then *invite* Jesus to draw near and *unburden* whatever isn't helpful. As a result, your anger will soften and your exile will finally get to rest.

Benefits, Dangers, Needs, and Fears

Now let's look at the benefits, dangers, needs, and fears associated with anger.

Benefits

Anger is a God-given emotion intended for your welfare. Like all other emotions, your anger doesn't need to be silenced; it needs to be heard. When treated as an ally, your anger can:

- point you to exiles needing your attention
- protect you from danger
- become your ambition or motivation
- fight for justice
- become the part of you that speaks honestly and points out difficult truths

Dangers

When your anger gets extreme, however, it can lead you into danger. Anger *will* express itself. The question is, when, where, and how? Without healthy internal boundaries, angry parts of you will surface in unhealthy ways, leading to problems such as:

- irritability and hostility toward others
- aggressive impulses or actions
- harshly judgmental attitudes toward yourself and others
- cynicism or bitterness
- physical tension
- swearing, yelling, and negativity

Needs

To stay within healthy boundary lines, your anger needs for you to:

- develop a comfortable distance from it so that you can help it find its rightful place in your internal family
- be open to another perspective
- be willing to be humble before God and open to his instructions on how best to proceed
- learn to pray that others with whom you are angry will be filled with the fruit of the Holy Spirit[2]

Fears

Like all other parts of your soul, your anger is trying to help you— even though its methods at first may be misguided. To help anger stay at a comfortable distance and become your ally, get to know its fears, such as:

- *No one will take care of what I'm protecting.*
- *My voice won't be heard.*
- *I won't be appreciated.*
- *The injustice I suffered won't be avenged.*

When you notice an angry thought or feeling taking over, view the uprising as an invitation to befriend this hurting part that's crying out for attention. If it's crowding your Spirit-led self, listen with curiosity and gently ask it to step back so you can better understand it—and tend to the hurting part of your soul it defends. Let your anger know you care and are taking the lead.

MANIFESTATIONS OF ANGER

Church pews are filled with people like Gabe who want to be loving people but don't know how. In fact, domestic violence is so common that the law doesn't even require us, as therapists, to report it. You may not want to be angry, but angry parts can be stubborn. When working with your anger, identify whether its target is (1) others, (2) yourself, or (3) God.

Anger Toward Others: Passive and Aggressive Parts

What do you do when you're furious inside? What happens when an injustice has occurred? Gabe would either yell or sleep. Like him, you might go into *fight* mode in a counterproductive way. If you're overtaken by your anger, you can become aggressive, taking justice into your own hands. Or you might take *flight*, carrying the burdens of judgmental thoughts and resentful feelings along with you. If you're passive and don't advocate for yourself, you're not honoring yourself as a person made in the image of God.

The path to meaningful relationships and abundant living involves pausing when you want to fight or take flight, honoring the part of you that's angry, and offering the time and space it needs to gain perspective. It also means praying for that part of yourself and asking God to help it see as he sees. Once that part of you feels witnessed and understood, you can determine what action to take on its behalf. You might want to speak calmly on behalf of your anger to the person who hurt you. You can also become intentional about channeling anger's power in productive ways. Once you befriend your anger, you'll be able to lead it in taking appropriate action.

Anger Toward Self: The Inner Critic

How do you deal with anger toward yourself? I, Kim, had a client who didn't see the harm in berating herself. So I asked her if she would talk to her children that way. She paused for a moment and replied, "If I talked to my children the way I talk to myself, I would be reported to the Department of Child Protective Services!"

You, too, may have an inner critic that drags you down, a voice inside that says things you wouldn't say to your worst enemy: *You worthless idiot! Why do you always do that?* If so, you've met your inner critic, the part of you that thrives on letting you know about every little thing you could've done better. Your inner critic is a protector. It has the good intention of trying to help you do your best, but its strategy is limited and keeps you from experiencing the compassionate presence of your Spirit-led self. If you notice this angry part berating you, ask it to give you just a little space. Then take time to focus on it and befriend it. What are its fears if it doesn't do its job? Connect with this critic and invite it to become your champion instead.

Anger Toward God: Resentful Parts

You might love God and know he wants what's best for you. And yet parts of you may carry resentment toward him. Perhaps you've lost a loved one and asked, *How could God take that special person from me?* You may have been treated unfairly. Or you may feel that your life's achievements just never measure up.

You tell yourself that God is good all the time, that he means well for you, and that he's working out things for your good. But a part of you doesn't buy it and has made up its own story: *Why bother praying? God doesn't care. Does he enjoy watching me suffer?*

A part of you may be carrying belief-burdens like these. If so, you may rebel against God or descend into self-pity. If any part of you is struggling with these feelings, take a You-Turn: *focus, befriend, invite, unburden,* and recruit that renegade to *integrate* with your soul's faithful team of rivals.

GOD PUT BOUNDARIES ON CHAOS

Anger can feel chaotic, and so can other emotions. The task is to let God help you put boundaries around your chaotic feelings. Like the Old Testament prophet Jonah, you can become so overwhelmed by bitterness, for example, that your life spirals into chaos. But just as God contained chaos "in the beginning," with his help you can grow to love the most difficult parts of your soul and find that "the boundary lines [fall] . . . in pleasant places" (Ps. 16:6).

The book of Genesis teaches that in the beginning, "The earth was without form and void, and darkness was over the face of the deep" (Gen. 1:2 ESV). The Hebrew words for *formless* and *void* can be translated as "emptiness" or "chaos," and signify purposelessness and despair in our lives. In the biblical creation narrative, God set a boundary by creating light: "And God said, 'Let there be light' . . . And God separated the light from the darkness. God called the light Day, and the darkness he called Night" (Gen. 1:3, 4–5 ESV). God took what had been chaos and established the beautiful rhythm of day and night.

After limiting the darkness, God created another epic boundary when he said, "Let the water under the sky be gathered to one place, and let dry ground appear" (Gen. 1:9). In the ancient Near East, the Hebrew word for *waters* again could be understood to mean "chaos" and could signify anger and destruction.[3] In the creation story, the source of chaos is not identified. But we do learn that the power of God's spoken word placed boundaries around chaos, allowing the dry land to exist in harmony with the water. As God separated light from darkness and the waters from the dry land, he can establish boundaries within your soul. He can take your anger and despair and turn them into something beautiful.

EVEN THE WIND AND THE WAVES OBEY HIM

Your anger, when transformed in the presence of your Spirit-led self, can remind you that you have more power than you know. As your anger finds its God-given role, it can help you effect positive change in your soul—change that will benefit you, your family, your workplace, and your community. Should your anger stem from suffering personal pain or injustice, it may prompt you to join a ministry or start a social enterprise to help others who have suffered a similar wrong. Instead of causing you to feel stuck, your anger can offer guidance and become one of your wisest consultants and greatest allies.

> As your anger finds its God-given role, it can help you effect positive change in your soul—change that will benefit you, your family, your workplace, and your community.

One time Jesus was on a boat with some friends. Suddenly, a raging storm moved in, and the waves started flooding the boat. At Jesus' command, the winds and waves died down. Just as he stilled the waves in the creation narrative and that day on the boat with his friends, he can be the "I" in the center of your storm.[4] Remember the words of the classic hymn: "Be still, my soul; the waves and winds still know / His voice who ruled them while He dwelt below."[5]

Chapter 10

BOUNDARIES WITH FEAR AND ANXIETY

*Try to keep your small, fearful self close to you. . . .
Let it teach you its wisdom; let it tell you that you
can live instead of just surviving. Gradually you will
become one, and you will find that Jesus is living
in your heart and offering you all you need.*
—Henri Nouwen, *The Inner Voice of Love*

*For God did not give us a spirit of timidity or cowardice
or fear, but [He has given us a spirit] of power and of love
and of sound judgment and personal discipline [abilities
that result in a calm, well-balanced mind and self-control].*
—2 Timothy 1:7 (AMP)

fear
ˈfir/
noun
"an unpleasant emotion caused by the threat of danger, pain,
or harm"[1]

anx·i·e·ty

aNGˈzīədē/

noun

"a feeling of worry, nervousness, or unease about something with an uncertain outcome"[2]

WHAT IF WE told you it takes fear to have courage?

Think of the thing that frightens you most. Moses, for example, a hero of faith, feared the call on his life to lead a great nation out of slavery and into the Promised Land. Overcome by the fearful part of himself, he gave God several reasons why he couldn't obey: he doubted himself, he feared rejection by the people God had asked him to lead, and he didn't speak fluently; in fact, he may have had a speech impediment (Ex. 4:1–10). Moses had real fears that he brought to God, and God answered them one by one. God responded to Moses' fear, not with a platitude or a pep talk, but with a promise to stay near: "I will be with you" (Ex. 3:12). Eventually Moses liberated the Hebrew nation from a tyrannical pharaoh. You, too, can do mighty things in the spiritual realm when you face your fears.

In general, where are you in relation to fear? How about anxiety? Put a mark on the graph below to indicate your answer for both emotions:

Too Close————————Comfortable Distance————————Too Far

MEGAN TAKES A YOU-TURN WHEN SHE FEELS ANXIETY

As we saw in chapters 2 and 3, Megan's striving task manager was causing tension in her relationship with her husband. Her well-intended protector would prioritize Megan's never-ending to-do list above almost anything else, including having meaningful conversations with her spouse and enjoying time with her children. I, Kim, sought to help Megan take a You-Turn with this hardworking part.

Focus and Befriend

As we began, I asked Megan to close her eyes and tell me where in her body she was carrying her striving task manager part. She said she felt it in her shoulders, which just happened to be all hunched up. Inviting her to practice Spirit-led self-leadership and to use her God-given imagination, I asked her if she could envision this hardworking part. Closing her eyes and pausing for a moment, Megan replied that she could imagine herself walking up an "eternal escalator," carrying heavy buckets of water in both hands. This part said to her:

I'm lazy if I'm not working.
People are counting on me to bring order and structure.
How can I give myself time to rest?

"How do you feel toward this task manager with so many fears?" I asked.

Megan replied, "I hate it! I want it to go away. It's wrecking my marriage!"

"It makes sense that a part of you doesn't like your task manager. Do you think you could notice that critical part and ask it to step back? You might want to let it know that your task manager will become calm when you connect to it from a place of compassion," I said.

From her Spirit-led self, Megan asked this critical part to give her some space. She then was able to befriend her internal task manager and welcome it to speak freely. As a result, she felt more peaceful.

Invite and Unburden

Though I knew Megan had been a Christian for many years, I asked whether Jesus was near her task manager part. Megan replied that it knew *about* him, but it didn't sense his presence. She embraced the idea of inviting the anxious part of her soul to get to know him better. I said a prayer, then asked if she could imagine Jesus near this burdened part. After some silence, she said yes. In her mind's eye the escalator had disappeared, and she had put down the buckets of water.

"We're sitting together," she said. "I feel light, strong, and . . . *still.* I have a new feeling of taking in God's love without having to do anything."

As Megan felt calmer, she gained access to the exiled fear this anxious task manager had been protecting. And, as is common, this exile started showing her a memory.

"When I was eight years old, we lived in a nice neighborhood, but ours was the smallest house on the block," she said. "Sometimes at night I would walk around outside and look into the windows of the big houses. In my mind, I can see a window I used to look into a lot. Inside were two armchairs facing each other and a clean, white carpet. My carpet looks nothing like that—it's a mess because of my boys."

I asked Megan if she sensed Jesus' nearness to the fearful part of herself. At first she said she couldn't. I then asked if the part wanted Jesus to draw near, and Megan nodded her head. We prayed to invite Jesus to be close and, after some moments of quiet, I asked if she could sense his presence. Megan replied, "Yes, he is like the sun shining on me."

"What's happening now?" I asked.

"I'm imagining that we're leaving the window and walking down a path together. I feel lighter. I'm realizing that I like my living room carpet covered with toys because it reminds me of my kids," she said.

I asked Megan if she wanted to update her eight-year-old part with all that she had learned and how she had grown since she was a little girl. She said this fearful part became happier when it noticed how mature she is now.

"What does she think of you, of who you've become?"

"She's happy that I'm doing all the things I always wanted to do—that I have a job and a wonderful family. And she's realizing my life is more fun than what was happening (*or not happening*) in those empty living rooms!"

Returning to Megan's task manager, I asked if Jesus wanted to give this hardworking part a gift. After a long pause, she simply said, "Being still together." Softly, she asked him when she could stop working so hard. In her heart, he answered, *Do what you can, and then let the rest go. I am with you no matter what.*

Megan then commented, "There's less water in the buckets now. Much of that water came from the idea that I had to do it all. Now I know that I only have to do what I can. Responsibility for the whole world is not in my hands."

Integrate

"What new role would your task manager like to play now?" I asked.

"It wants to let me know when it's time to slow down," she replied.

Megan's hardworking part had held the extreme belief that she should never rest, never play, never stop working. Now, having a broader perspective, Megan's striving task manager wanted to become her trusted adviser and alert her when it was time to rest.

At our final session, Megan walked into my office more casually than in the early days of our work together. She didn't need to launch into a litany of issues, because I already knew her well—and she had grown to understand herself with compassion.

Instead, she told me about how she had been home one night

and decided to put off loading the dishwasher because she wanted to spend time playing cards with her family. For her, playing cards was a giant step. She laughed as she said to me, "I can't believe it! Out of habit, I was aware of the dishes the whole time, but my faithful new adviser kept reminding me how important it is to relax with my husband and kids!"

Summary of Megan's You-Turn

To take a You-Turn, Megan first *focused* on where she was feeling physical tension (in her shoulders). Closing her eyes and engaging her God-given capacity for creativity, she imagined her task manager as an image of herself walking up an "eternal escalator." To *befriend* this striving part of her soul, Megan listened and prayerfully imagined a younger, exiled part that had picked up extreme beliefs when looking into others' windows as a child. We realized that her anxious manager was trying to meet the needs of this fearful exile. Soon Megan *invited* Jesus to be with this part that was carrying the fear of her family's uncertain future.

Megan's burden was the meaning that a young part of her had created as a result of growing up in a smaller house than her prosperous neighbors. This part of her had developed the belief that a large house equals a happy life. *Unburdening* followed when her exiled part drew near to Jesus. Megan said she felt "lighter" because that belief-burden was now gone. She gained fresh perspective, realizing that happiness wasn't just about the success she had achieved. She now related better with her striving task manager and shifted her focus to spending time with her husband and children. Megan's unburdening freed her to move forward, building her life as a Spirit-led woman.

Finally, during the *integration* step, Megan's previously anxious part took on the different task of letting her know when she needed to rest. Moving forward, Megan resolved to listen to her new, trusted adviser, recognizing its invaluable role of reminding her when it was time to relax her shoulders, set aside her to-do list, and enjoy resting and playing with her family.

GETTING TO KNOW FEAR AND ANXIETY

Just as Megan addressed her anxiety and fear, so can you. To begin, consider the difference between these two related emotions. It might help to think of fear as an exile with a specific, present concern: this vulnerable part of your internal family might fear being hurt, rejected, powerless, or physically unsafe. Once identified, you can calm your fear.

The problem is that we all tend to avoid facing our fears. And that's when anxiety steps in as a protector. Unlike fear, anxiety is chaotic, future-oriented, and creative. It thinks up all kinds of things for you to worry about, things that may have no bearing on your current reality. In doing so, your anxiety protects you from facing the real things you fear by keeping you *distracted*. It's often easier to dwell on the things that *might* happen than to implement a plan to counter real threats.

Your exiled fear doesn't need to be starved or shunned; it needs to be understood. But to befriend your fear, befriend your anxiety first. Let's look at the benefits, dangers, needs, and concerns associated with the anxiety at work within your soul.

Benefits, Dangers, Needs, and Concerns

Benefits
When respected as a valuable part of your soul, your anxiety can:

- signal the presence of a fearful exile needing your attention
- inform you of emotional, spiritual, and physical challenges that need to be faced

- protect you by warning you of things that might go wrong
- help you be more careful
- be sensitive to change and help you plan ahead
- become the part of you that acts courageously, humbly leading others
- remind you that you're a perceptive, tender soul

Dangers

Anxiety *will* express itself. The question is, when, where, and how? When your anxiety becomes extreme, ironically it can create the very dangers you're trying to avoid. Without healthy internal boundaries, your anxiety will surface in troubling ways, such as:

- physical limitations (shortness of breath, lightheadedness, or sleeplessness, for example)
- insecurity
- inordinate people-pleasing
- inability to focus or concentrate
- feelings of chaos or being out of control
- internal chatter, confusion, or chronic worry
- hypervigilance
- catastrophizing, such that problems seem bigger than they are
- panic attacks

Needs

To stay within healthy boundary lines, your anxiety needs:

- to develop courage, with God's help
- for you to help it recognize that it is only one part of you— not the sum total of who you are
- for you to lovingly remind it of the truth of God's power

Fears

Like every internal protector, your anxiety wants to help—even though its methods at first may be misguided and counter-productive. To help your anxiety stay within healthy boundary lines and become your ally, get to know its concerns about letting your Spirit-led self take the lead, such as:

- *I'll put myself in danger.*
- *I won't be prepared.*
- *I'll mishandle a responsibility.*
- *I'll be rejected and alone.*
- *I'll disappoint someone.*
- *I've taken on too much.*

If you notice anxiety in your life, take a You-Turn and *focus* on this anxious part that's crying out for your attention. If it's taking you over, listen and befriend it. It will relax and transform into a helpful adviser when it knows your Spirit-led self is there, leading the way.

MANIFESTATIONS OF FEAR AND ANXIETY

It's helpful to group anxious parts into three common categories: worrying and controlling parts, people-pleasing parts, and doubting parts. Consider the root fears that tend to lie behind each one.

Fear of the Unknown: Worry and Control

My, Alison's, client Steve worried about everything: He worried that if he didn't marry, he would grow old alone—and that if he were to marry, his wife would end up cheating on him. He worried that if he stayed in his job, he would burn out—and that if he left his job, he would never find another one. And ironically, Steve's unhappiness was *not* something Steve thought much about! The truth was Steve had never addressed the painful events in his past. Instead, his worrying manager kept him distracted by focusing on problems that didn't exist. If, like Steve, worry is driving your life, it's time to set some gentle boundaries with your worry and listen to your fear.

In Steve's case, worry kept him passive. In other cases, worry manifests as a desire to control—sometimes aggressively—your relationships, your work, or other areas of your life to ward off any possible danger or perceived threat. Your urge to control the people around you may lead to manipulation, abuse of power, or boundary violations. For example, a family came to see me, Alison, concerned about their fourteen-year-old daughter, Lindsey, who was showing a "rebellious" streak. I soon discovered that the mom, Diane, wouldn't let her daughter out of their home unless she was with an adult or at school. When Diane was a young child she had nearly been abducted by strangers while playing outside by herself. Now, as a mom, she was terrified that something bad might happen to her own child. A controlling manager constantly warned her, *You must vigilantly monitor Lindsey's every move.* Though well intended, Diane's controlling impulse was encroaching on her daughter's need to become more independent.

Diane was able to befriend her propensity to control, and she invited Jesus to be near the traumatized exile this manager was protecting. With his help, she could calm herself when she feared for her daughter's safety: *The world may not be safe, but God wants me to put my trust in him.* Together, Diane and her daughter negotiated new rules that took into account both of their needs.

Pay attention if you have a worried part, either passive or controlling, that eclipses your Spirit-led self. It might indeed keep you safe. You might also miss out, though, on the joys of adventure and intimacy.

Thankfully, there's another way. It starts with befriending your worry and gently helping it step back so you can get to the real source of your need. Acknowledge that part's good intention to keep you and the ones you love safe. Once you befriend your worry from your Spirit-led self, you'll be able to give it the care it needs so that it stays within healthy boundaries in your soul. Then you can invite God to be near the fearful exile it protects and provide the comfort and practical help it needs.

Fear of Rejection: People-Pleaser Parts

Exiled fear of losing others' love often leads one to develop a protective people-pleaser part. Your internal people-pleaser, sensitive to the needs of others as it might be, needs gentle boundaries too. If its pleasing actions stem from a fear of rejection buried deep inside, the part won't truly be giving out of love for others. In this case, this pleasing part of you is *too close*. On the other hand, if you don't care at all what others think, then this part of you might be *too far*. Focus, befriend, and thus gain some perspective about your inner people-pleaser when it becomes extreme—you'll then be able to attend to the precious exile hiding underneath.

Signs that you have a people-pleaser part might be:

- not saying no when no is needed
- feeling resentful of the very people you're working overtime to please
- telling a white lie to ward off an angry reaction

When you're pleasing others to avoid conflict, you're not giving voice to your fear. That's the time to focus on what's keeping you from bravely expressing your needs. Once you befriend the part of yourself that's pleasing others out of fear, you'll be able to lead yourself through honest conversations and develop deeper, more genuine relationships with others. You can set gentle boundaries with your inner people-pleaser and extend loving compassion to the fearful part of you not wanting to let others down. Imagine the freedom of releasing the burden of feeling that you need to please everyone—and replacing it with a humble acceptance of your human limitations.

Fear of Trusting God: Doubt

Some of the giants of our Christian faith—those known for heroic acts of faithful obedience—struggled with menacing doubt. Mother Teresa, who devoted her life to caring for the poorest of the poor out of love for God, described her doubt this way:

> Where is my faith?—even deep down, right in, there is nothing but emptiness and darkness. My God—how painful is this unknown pain. It pains without ceasing. I have no faith. I dare not utter the words and thoughts that crowd in my heart and make me suffer untold agony. So many unanswered questions live within me—I am afraid to uncover them—because of the blasphemy. If there be God, please forgive me.[3]

Though her journals reflected years of struggling with doubt, Mother Teresa chose to invite Jesus to draw near to her pain. She served him until the end of her days, writing: "Here I am Lord, with joy I accept all to the end of my life—and I will smile at Your Hidden Face—always."[4] What do you do when your doubt is crowding your heart and you're afraid to acknowledge unanswered questions?

Christian author C. S. Lewis offers a way through the dilemma of doubt. Faith expressed as obedience, he said, even in the face of doubt, is a powerful

Imagine the freedom of releasing the burden of feeling that you need to please everyone—and replacing it with a humble acceptance of your human limitations.

spiritual move. He conveyed the contours of his own doubt (and faith) when he composed *The Screwtape Letters*. This classic takes the form of a series of letters from an elder demon to his nephew, Wormwood. One message from Uncle Screwtape to Wormwood reveals how the greatest threat to the powers of darkness would not be possible without an element of doubt. "Our cause is never more in danger" he wrote, "than when a human, no longer desiring, but still intending, to do . . . [God's] will, looks round upon a universe from which every trace of him seems to have vanished and asks why he has been forsaken, and still obeys."[5] What if your doubt, like Lewis's, could transform into courage and become your faithful companion on your lifelong journey toward obedience?

TURNING FEAR AND ANXIETY INTO ALLIES

Your fear and anxiety, when transformed in the presence of your Spirit-led self, can become faithful servants in your internal family. When they make themselves known, befriend them and listen to them from your Spirit-led self. They can remind other, more self-sufficient parts of you that it's time to ask for help—that you don't have to face your challenges alone.

Let your fear and anxiety prompt you to invite Jesus to draw near, strengthening your faith. Without these two powerful emotions, you wouldn't have the opportunity to become courageous and faithful, to rise above and show God that he matters more to you than your circumstance—that you trust in him. When befriended, fear can lead to an abiding dependence on Jesus and a deeply satisfying intimacy with him.

Get to the root of your fear, underneath the chaos of anxiety. *A part of me is frightened* are powerful words to say as you draw near to God and live from your Spirit-led self. As with Moses, God may not take away your fear. But he will strengthen you with courage as you trust in him. The parts of your soul that have known anxiety and fear can become your beloved companions as you faithfully embrace what is, in the words of poet Mary Oliver, your "one wild and precious life."[6]

Chapter 11

BOUNDARIES WITH SADNESS

*There are many things that can only be
seen through eyes that have cried.*
—Archbishop Óscar Romero of San Salvador

*The Lord is near to the brokenhearted
and saves the crushed in spirit.*
—Psalm 34:18 (esv)

sad
săd
adjective
"affected by unhappiness or grief; sorrowful or mournful"[1]

You need your pain. Grief makes you real, and disappointment makes you resilient. Heartache fueled the creativity of
Kierkegaard, Beethoven, and Van Gogh, for example, and countless other luminaries throughout history. Vision, innovation, and
dependence on the Spirit are born from suffering. The pain of
our clients has driven them to seek Jesus and rise to new spiritual heights. Likewise, your sorrow can inspire new chapters of
purpose and creativity in your life.

Our work gives us a close-up view of the pain people carry.

155

The woman whose husband ignores her. The man whose wife and daughter died. The patient who struggles daily with the limitations of a chronic illness. The student who fears she'll never find herself—or someone to love. When nothing is working and God feels absent, the silence can be excruciating.

Consider Elijah, the Old Testament prophet who performed miracles, including raising a child from the dead and calling forth fire to rain down from the sky. Yet even Elijah experienced profound sorrow and darkness in his soul, asking God, at one point, to end his life: "It is enough; now, O LORD, take away my life, for I am no better than my fathers" (1 Kings 19:4 ESV). Many of us have a part of our soul like Elijah that is so overcome with sorrow we lose sight of God's power.

"How can we respond to this brokenness?" Henri Nouwen asked in his beautiful book *Life of the Beloved*. And he answered by portraying the painful aspects of life as a faithful offering: "I'd like to suggest two ways: first, befriending it, and, second, putting it under the blessing."[2] No matter the cause of your pain, your heart can become a reservoir of compassion and empathy for others. To paraphrase Nouwen, through your experience of suffering, you can be taken, blessed, broken—and given for the world.

In general, where are you in relation to your sadness? Put a mark on the graph below to indicate your answer:

Too Close————————Comfortable Distance————————Too Far

ANDREA TAKES A YOU-TURN WHEN SHE FEELS SADNESS

Andrea, a thirtysomething math teacher, came to see me, Alison, a few weeks after learning of her fiance's infidelity, downcast eyes belying her smile. A capable woman known for her cheerful demeanor and can-do mentality, Andrea hated feeling sad.

Focus and Befriend

"What is wrong with me? I have so many crazy emotions," Andrea said, smoothing the crease in her pressed pencil skirt. "I can't stop crying, but then I feel so angry. I don't know what to do with myself."

"Can you take a moment and focus on the part of yourself that's understandably angry, Andrea?" I asked. "What would it like you to know?"

Andrea paused and checked in with her angry part. "It's afraid that the sadness will overwhelm me," she confided. "What if I can't stop crying?"

Aware that Andrea's anger was protecting a grief-stricken exile, I asked, "Can you let your anger know that we won't let the sadness overwhelm you? We want to get to know it and give it the care it needs. Is there anything your anger needs to help it give you some space so you can spend some time with your sadness?"

Andrea thought for a moment and replied, "It wants to know that I'll cry only for a little while and then move on with my day."

"That seems fair. What amount of time seems reasonable to your anger?" I asked.

"I think if I could set aside a few hours this coming weekend to talk to friends and journal, that would be a good start."

"Great!" I said. "Is it okay with your angry part to spend the remainder of our time together today with your sadness?"

"Yes, my anger feels good about that," she said with all sincerity. "It feels relieved that you'll be here to help me keep the boundary."

Now that Andrea's sadness had our attention, the tears she had been stifling began streaming down her face. I checked in with Andrea to see if her sorrow was overwhelming her, and she assured me that it was not. "It feels good to finally cry," she said.

"What would your sadness like you to know?"

"Sam was an angel to me when we first met. He was my first love. My own dad left my mom and me, but Sam stayed close. He promised me a life that would be different—full of love and laughter. I felt so much security and stability with him. Over the past year, he has changed. I can see it now. But I just can't believe he's throwing it all away."

Invite and Unburden

Andrea seemed calmer now, though tears still cascaded down her cheeks: "I still love Sam, and it's hard to explain, but I feel like I can't be whole without him."

"It sounds like your sad part has picked up a belief-burden that you can't be whole unless Sam is in your life. Did I understand you correctly?"

"Yes," she said. "I know that's crazy, because our relationship's been difficult lately, but some part of me feels like I need him to survive."

"I'm curious whether you sense that Jesus is near as you share this very real concern that you may not be able to survive without Sam."

Andrea quietly nodded and said that she sensed Jesus' presence. "He's reminding me that though Sam has changed and our relationship is broken, the good that was there can't ever be taken away from me. The love he showed me and the kindness that I glimpsed . . . they were imperfect in him but reflections of what I can always find in God."

From her Spirit-led self, Andrea *invited* Jesus to be near the sad part of her that bravely bore the weight of her false belief. Once Jesus drew near, Andrea *unburdened* as she recognized that God's love—not Sam's—made her whole. Did she still feel sad?

Certainly. But she also felt empowered to move forward a stronger, freer young woman.

Integrate

"Andrea, how is your angry protector part responding to what just happened?" I asked.

"It's much calmer now," she said as she wiped her eyes, her facial expression reassuringly congruent with her words.

"Is there a new role this anger would like to take on, now that it's able to relax?" I asked.

"Moving forward, my anger can help me advocate for myself when communicating with Sam," she replied thoughtfully. "It liked when you suggested that my sadness didn't have to overwhelm me. My anger wants me to speak on behalf of my sadness. It can help me be strong when I let him know how much he's hurt me."

The angry and sad parts of Andrea had been vying for control. When *integrating* them, Andrea realized her anger wanted to take on a new role. As an advocate, it could help her speak with strength on behalf of her sadness. She no longer felt chaotic internally.

Summary of Andrea's You-Turn

When Andrea took a You-Turn and focused on her sadness, an angry part of her stepped in to protest the idea, not wanting her to be overwhelmed by it. Leading from her Spirit-led self, Andrea negotiated with her anger, helping it understand that she would set gentle boundaries with her grief. In doing so, she learned that her sadness didn't want to overwhelm her. It simply wanted to be acknowledged as valid. As Andrea grew in compassion for her sadness, she was able to differentiate from it and create a gentle boundary around it in her heart. Like a small, hurting child, it needed her presence and the security of loving containment. Andrea had been afraid of her sorrow and so had tried to keep it away. Ironically, when she befriended it and let it come in a little closer, she didn't feel overwhelmed by it. Instead, she felt calmer.

GETTING TO KNOW YOUR SADNESS

How is your relationship with the part of yourself that feels deep sorrow? If your sadness is too close, you might experience loneliness, self-pity, and depression. If your sadness is too far, however, you may deny the reality of this important emotion. Like Andrea, you may have an angry protector striving valiantly to keep your sadness at bay. Either way, your sadness needs your care. Become curious about it, listen to it, and befriend it from your Spirit-led self.

Your sadness needs your care. Become curious about it, listen to it, and befriend it from your Spirit-led self.

Are you mourning the loss of a person or a dream? How you process this experience will determine its effect on your life. If your suffering has become your identity, it's too close to you. Create a sacred space for suffering in your heart, and it will make you more like Christ.

Benefits, Dangers, Needs, and Fears

Now, let's look at the benefits, dangers, needs, and fears associated with feeling sadness.

Benefits

Painful loss deserves to be honored and offered up to God. When treated as an ally, the part of you carrying sadness can:

- remind you of your need for others and for God
- help you become aware of a personal loss or burden that needs to be examined

- help you understand your heart and the things you deeply love
- help you develop empathy and come alongside others who are suffering
- speak the truth of your story and the hardships you've faced

Dangers

Sadness *will* make its presence known. The question is, when, where, and how? Like all other emotions, your sadness increases when swept aside. The more extreme it becomes, the more likely it will lead you into danger. If not lovingly welcomed, your sadness will surface in unhealthy ways, leading to:

- feelings of being invisible, worthless, or unlovable
- depression and despair
- weariness and exhaustion
- rumination about painful memories
- insecurity, false guilt, and chronic shame

Needs

To stay within healthy boundary lines, your sadness needs:

- a safe place to grieve the people, relationships, or opportunities you've lost
- validation of the sorrow it holds (versus a quick fix)
- a gentle boundary so it can find its rightful place in your internal family and become your sacred companion

Fears

Like all other aspects of yourself, the part of you holding on to painful memories or the loss of dreams serves a purpose—even though your protectors may not yet understand its value. To assist your sadness in becoming your ally and staying within proper boundary lines, get to know its fears about letting your Spirit-led self take the lead. Some examples of these fears are:

- *If I move forward with my life, the deceased loved one I'm mourning might be forgotten.*
- *Forgiving implies that my pain never happened.*
- *Exposing my sadness will drive people even farther away.*
- *No one will pay attention to me if I'm not in need.*

When a person or situation threatens to overwhelm you, take a You-Turn. Focus on the sorrowful part of yourself needing your attention. If it's too close, listen well. Show up and ask it to give you a little space so you can get to know it better. If it's too far away, invite it in closer so that you can learn more about it. As the part of you carrying sadness develops trust in God, made known through the loving attention of your Spirit-led self, this lost sheep wandering in your soul will settle into the arms of the Good Shepherd (John 10:7–10).

There's a difference between moving on and moving forward. You may never forget about your loss. As you befriend your sadness, though, you can move forward on your journey to an abundant life.

CAUSES OF YOUR SADNESS

It's helpful to think of the causes of sadness in three categories: sadness as a response to the loss of something good, the loss of something bad, and the loss of what might have been.[3]

Sorrow in Response to Losing What Was Good

Loss pervades our human existence. If you haven't known loss, then you haven't known love. Most of us have known both. You might have had to leave a city and friends that you love. Or perhaps you're mourning a fractured relationship or one that ended. Maybe you're silently grieving the death of a parent, sibling, or child.

When I, Alison, was in my twenties, my parents sold the house of my childhood and moved far away. I had lived every day of my first eighteen years in that house, just down the street from my grandparents and a few miles from the church and schools that had shaped everything about me. At the time, I acknowledged the change as unavoidable and thought I had "moved on." But the loss of this tight-knit community caught up to me several years later in my thirties when I started wanting to put down roots. My exiled sadness overwhelmed me, and I started longing to see my childhood home. Miranda Lambert sings poignantly about this exact feeling in "The House That Built Me."[4]

> As the part of you carrying sadness develops trust in God, made known through the loving attention of your Spirit-led self, this lost sheep wandering in your soul will settle into the arms of the Good Shepherd.

The next summer, I returned to my hometown for the first time in years and parked in front of my old house. Something inside of me needed to grieve. I knocked on the door and asked the stranger who opened it if I could come in. I barely greeted her—my eyes welling with tears said enough. She graciously left me alone to walk through every room of that house, retracing precious memories with each step. Though filled with sadness, this bittersweet goodbye to my childhood home helped me reconnect with parts of my soul. I couldn't go back in time—nor did I really want to—but I could incorporate into my future what that home represented. To this day, my family and I spend time each summer "back home"—hiking in the mountains, chasing deer on my uncle's ranch, and revisiting beloved childhood friends. My life is more complete as a result of connecting to the sadness that overwhelmed my soul.

You don't have to be ambushed by a broken heart. You can listen to your sadness and lead it with compassion. Our usual tendency is to numb pain. But when you numb your pain, you numb joyful feelings too. Focusing on and befriending your sadness brings back to life parts of your soul that were frozen. It moves you forward into new hope and helps you recognize, and stay connected to, what matters most.

Joy and Sadness:
Two Sides of the Same Coin

Your soul holds joy and sadness. Both parts want to serve the good of the whole. Joy helps you laugh, and tears are vital to vibrant living too. Turn them off, and you become disconnected from precious aspects of your soul. Once you embrace your sadness, this important emotion can find a helpful role within your internal family. And your heart will develop empathy for others. The wise King Solomon said there is "a time to weep and a time to laugh, a time to mourn and a time to dance" (Eccl. 3:4). How wonderful that, by God's divine design, you can be truly joyful on one hand and be present to your sadness on the other!

Sorrow in Response to Losing What Was Bad

Sometimes it's hard to let go of people or patterns to which you have grown accustomed, even if they weren't good for you. In fact, leaving behind something in your life that's broken sometimes hurts more than leaving behind something good. Healthy goodbyes leave us with happy memories. We look back on those people or places with fondness and hold them in our hearts. We take the good with us, even if the person or place is in our past. But saying goodbye to destructive relationships can be extremely painful.

For example, I, Alison, worked with a bright, sincere woman, Maria, who had been dating an abusive, addicted man for four years. I asked Maria, "What keeps you from leaving?" Maria paused and then spoke honestly, "I don't want to face the pain." She had given four years of her life to loving someone who had hurt her repeatedly. A part of her didn't want to accept the reality that she had wasted so much time on a destructive, dead-end relationship. So she was choosing the pain she knew over the pain she didn't know—and was missing an opportunity to move forward with her life.

You don't have to be ruled by fear of facing the regret of past mistakes or lost years. If you're struggling to leave behind something that's broken, take a You-Turn and get to know your fear. Befriending your sorrow and providing it with the comfort of your Spirit-led self helps you move forward and start anew.

Sorrow in Response to Losing a Dream

In addition to befriending sadness about the loss of good and bad things in your life, give attention to the parts of you grieving the loss of dreams that can no longer materialize: a life curtailed by physical limitations or a happily-ever-after that never came true. Are you carrying disappointment about unfulfilled dreams and expectations? Does a gap exist between your hopes and the reality of life? Be present to the part of yourself grieving this loss, even as you say goodbye to what might have been.

TURNING SADNESS INTO YOUR ALLY

Sadness, when transformed in the presence of your Spirit-led self, becomes your compassion and strength. Pain becomes redemptive when it causes you to draw near to God and experience his power. The apostle Paul begged God to take away a "thorn in his flesh."

But God replied, "My grace is sufficient for you, for my power is made perfect in weakness" (2 Cor. 12:9). Paul understood that God wanted to shape his character and bring about spiritual fruit in his life more than he wanted Paul to be comfortable. When you befriend a sad part, God will use your pain to cultivate gentleness within your soul. Gentleness toward yourself leads to gentleness toward others and makes you more like Christ.

When you're experiencing the grief of a loss, create space in your life for mourning. Roughly a third of the Psalms express lament. Lament signifies faith, not weakness; it shows you're hanging on. Set an intention with yourself—that whenever you feel pain, you'll check in with your sad part and invite Jesus to draw near. The resulting connection matters so much now, as this grieving part of you experiences afresh God's loving-kindness. "Blessed are those who mourn, for they will be comforted" (Matt. 5:4).

Author Joni Eareckson Tada has turned the suffering of physical paralysis into a ministry to millions. She wrote, "Inner anguish . . . forces us to embrace God, out of desperate, urgent, need. . . . God is never closer than when your heart is aching."[5] Let your sorrow lead you to deeper union with the Savior so that as you are crucified with him, you also may be a healing presence in the world. "Humble yourselves under the mighty hand of God, that He may exalt you in due time, casting all your care upon Him, for He cares for you" (1 Peter 5:6–7 NKJV).

With the cross and resurrection of Jesus, God set in motion a series of unstoppable events that will redeem every last painful experience in your life. Until then the Spirit intercedes on your behalf. Romans 8:26 says, "The Spirit helps us in our weakness. We do not know what we ought to pray for, but the Spirit himself intercedes for us." He prays for you when you don't have the words. On your journey through this broken, beautiful life, may your sadness know the steadfast compassion of Jesus and become one of the most honored aspects of your soul.

Chapter 12

BOUNDARIES WITH ENVY AND DESIRE

Her beauty and the moonlight overthrew ya.
—Leonard Cohen, "Hallelujah"

*Praise the LORD, my soul, and forget not all his benefits
. . . who satisfies your desires with good things.*
—Psalm 103:2, 5

en·vy

en-vē

noun

"a painful or resentful awareness of an advantage enjoyed by another joined with a desire to possess the same advantage"[1]

de·sire

dē-ˈzī(-ə)r

noun

"a strong feeling of wanting to have something or wishing for something to happen"[2]

WHAT IF YOUR envy could help you realize your God-given potential? We've all looked over the fence and thought, *The grass is greener on the other side.* If your Spirit-led self doesn't step up to lead that envious part of your soul, you might find it poisoning your own grass—and your neighbor's lawn.

What issues make you feel envy? Whose grass is greener than yours? Or do you simply wish to have a "lawn" to call your own? Regardless, envy works to protect you from the pain of buried hopes and dreams, either by preventing pain (as in the case with managers) or by numbing it (as firefighters try to do).

In Genesis 37, we learn about Joseph and his brothers, sons of the biblical patriarch Jacob. Joseph's brothers envied Joseph because he was his father's favorite son. Even God seemed to favor him, too, by revealing to him in dreams the power he would have one day. Who wouldn't want to enjoy the feeling of being cherished by one's father or to receive visions straight from heaven of a grand future? But Joseph's brothers, instead of facing their desire to be cherished and honored, let envy stew in their hearts. In fact, they cooked up a plan to kill their younger brother. At the last minute, the eldest, feeling guilty, persuaded his siblings to sell Joseph into slavery instead of killing him. Nevertheless, they broke their father's heart.

Do you have an envious part that feels like Joseph's brothers did? Do you sometimes see another person's success and let it torment your soul? If so, take heart. You can *focus* on your envy and *befriend* it—it may even help you become your best self.

Think about your relationship to your envy and desire. In general, where are you in relation to them? Put a mark on the graph to indicate your answer:

Too Close————Comfortable Distance————Too Far

Let's look at how a client faced his desire for a woman he couldn't have—and how his envy motivated him to pursue a fulfilling relationship instead.

JOSÉ TAKES A YOU-TURN WHEN HE FEELS ENVY

José came to see me, Kim, because he couldn't get over the fact that the woman he loved was marrying another man. "I dated Amelia for years," he told me, "she just didn't know it!" Overwhelmed by years of longing for this unavailable woman, José felt trapped in a whirlwind of envy and unmet desire.

Focus on and Befriend the Protector

As we began our counseling work, I asked José more about his relationship with Amelia.

"I met her in an English class during our last semester at college," he said. "We had long conversations about the books we were reading. I'd never met anyone quite like her before. I knew she had a boyfriend, but she led me to think she cared for me. On the last day of class, she told me how much she'd enjoyed spending time together. These past few years, she's kept in touch with letters here and there. And she's even come to visit me. We have this incredible connection. I can't believe she's getting married."

"So, some part of you believed there was more there with Amelia, even though you knew she had a serious boyfriend?" I asked.

"Yes," José replied. "In some ways, knowing she was dating Matthew made me want her more. I wanted what he had," he said.

"How do you feel toward that part of you that envies Matthew?" I asked.

"I hate it," he replied. "Why can't I just move on and focus on another woman—one who is available? One who wants to be with me?"

"Could you extend compassion to your well-meaning inner critic, José?" I asked. "Let it know you appreciate its good intentions. And let it know that if we can get to know your envy, we might be able to help you develop a satisfying relationship."

When understood instead of criticized, José's envy was willing to relax. As José continued to focus on and befriend it, he learned that its role was to distract him by reminding him constantly about what others had. We soon came to realize that it was working hard to numb the pain of an exile.

Focus on and Befriend the Exile

The next time he came to see me, José had seen Amelia for the last time.

"I want to understand this part of myself that wants her to love me," José said, "even though I know she doesn't."

"José, could you focus for a moment on that desire?" I asked. "How do you feel toward that longing part of your soul?"

"I feel compassion," he said, "it's reminding me of when my mom dropped me off at my grandmother's and didn't come back."

As José connected to his desire from his Spirit-led self, he befriended it. He then started to realize that his biggest problem was not Amelia. Rather, he was overwhelmed by a desire to be loved, stemming from his grade school years when his mother, who struggled with addiction, had abandoned him. He was trying to heal by subconsciously re-creating a familiar situation and pursuing unavailable women.

Invite and Unburden

José continued to share the memories his exiled desire was showing him. Growing up, he had longed for his mother's presence.

After listening, I asked him if Jesus was near this part of him that was caught in the pain of the past.

José paused for a moment and then said, "I'm afraid if I invite Jesus to be near, I'll have to let my mom go. I'll have to let go of my hope that someday I'll be close to my mom."

"What does this part of you need from Jesus?" I asked.

"It wants him to know how much I long to be loved and how much it hurts that she left," José said, connecting to this exile. "I can see a light shining on this young part of me that has been longing for my mother all of these years. Jesus is with this part of me now," he shared after a few moments. "He understands."

José shared with me later that he had started praying for this part of himself. Using his prayerful imagination, he could see it coming out from the dark place where it had been hiding and stepping bravely into the light. As José invited Jesus to be near and unburdened the belief that he was insignificant, he received the knowledge that he was loved by God. He began to feel the joy of being alive and sensed himself beginning to dream.

Integrate

"Now that your desire is learning to step into the light of God's presence, is there another role your envy wants to have?" I asked José.

His answer came quickly: "It wants to remind me when I'm living in the past."

Months later José reported that he had met someone new. He was taking steps toward developing a meaningful relationship for the first time in his life.

Summary of José's You-Turn

As José began to *focus on* and *befriend* his envy, it relaxed. It had been too close, but on receiving his compassion it settled at a comfortable distance from his Spirit-led self. José then gained access to the exiled desire that his envy had stepped in to protect.

As José befriended this exile, he *invited* Jesus to be near. It then received Jesus' love and *unburdened* its painful belief. As a result, he stopped longing for someone he couldn't have. Instead, his envy became a signifier to him that there was some part needing to work through more grief from the past. Eventually, José stopped pursuing unavailable women and opened his heart in healthy ways to authentic love. From this Spirit-led place, he began to live in his God-given potential.

Like José, you can learn from parts of your soul when their strategies have backfired. Instead of making unsatisfying life choices, you can develop a healthy relationship with your envy and the unmet desire it has been protecting.

GETTING TO KNOW ENVY

Your envy gets a bad rap for all its valiant work on behalf of your exiles. With a little attention, envy can become your ally, prompting you to invite Jesus to minister to and redirect your desires. Recognizing that your Spirit-led self cares for it compassionately, this imposing part will gain trust in your ability to lead it. As you practice Spirit-led self-leadership, your envy can advocate for exiles waiting for you to befriend them.

When you do, you'll finally address the unmet desire that envy has been serving so faithfully over the years. And when you start to look at desire, you may stumble upon another part of yourself that carries the grief of loss or regret. As you get to know your desire, welcome the grief you encounter too. Embracing your grief helps you process it and harness the power of your desire to inform your life choices. Instead of envying someone else's "greener grass," you'll start enjoying the beauty growing right in front of you and watering your own lawn.

So, when you start to feel the curse of comparison, put your devoted envy to work for you: *Focus* on it and *befriend* it, appreciating its good intentions. *Invite* Jesus to be with it, *unburdening* its false beliefs. And if you follow the Five Steps with the desire your envy protects, you can *integrate* these two valuable parts of your soul into a team of (former) rivals.

Benefits, Dangers, Needs, and Fears

Consider the benefits, dangers, needs, and fears associated with feeling envy.

Benefits

Think of envy as a signpost, pointing you to areas of your life that need your attention. The presence of this feeling gives you clues about the state of your soul and alerts you to growth opportunities. Like all other emotions, your envy doesn't want to be shoved aside, but rather heard and understood. When treated as an ally, your envy can:

- lead you to longings you've ignored or denied
- alert you to a vulnerable part of your soul that might be feeling neglected
- help you become realistic about your limitations so you can move forward with realistic goals
- reveal unrealized potential within you
- learn from the successes of others

Dangers

The quickest way to lose your appreciation for something special is to compare it to something that seems better. Envy causes terrible damage if ruling your heart. Envy *will* express itself. The question is, when, where, and how? Without healthy internal boundaries, your envy surfaces in unhealthy ways and leads to:

- petty attitudes, anger, bullying, or hatred toward other people
- attempts or desires to thwart other people's happiness
- stealing and cheating
- distraction from your life's purpose
- failure to acknowledge legitimate desires
- isolation and missed opportunities to serve others and build community

Needs

To stay within healthy boundary lines, your envy needs to:

- learn to give you some space so you can gain clear perspective
- offer your resentment openhandedly to God, inviting him to shape your longings
- learn to trust your Spirit-led self so it can assume a more helpful role in your internal family

Fears

Like all other parts of you, your envy is trying to help you—even though its methods may be misguided. To help your envy stay within healthy boundary lines and become a helpful member of your internal family, get to know its fears about letting your Spirit-led self take the lead. Some examples of those fears may be:

- *I'll be stifled by heartache the rest of my life.*
- *My desires will be forgotten or ignored.*
- *I'll always be unhappy.*
- *I'll be bored if I don't get what I want.*

When you extend compassion to your envy, it loses its power over you. Then, as you gain clarity about the deeper desire it's protecting, you're able to redirect its energy into pursuing noble dreams. When it learns to trust your Spirit-led self, your envy can become your champion, cheering you on as you stay focused on building your life.

ENVY VS. JEALOUSY

In some instances, a feeling akin to envy—jealousy, to be precise—isn't necessarily out of line. Whereas envy longs for something that isn't rightfully yours, jealousy is the desire to possess what *is* rightfully yours.[3] For example, a wife rightly feels jealousy when her husband has an affair. Jealousy was God's response when his chosen people, the nation of Israel, repeatedly turned from him throughout history.[4] In fact, Exodus 34:14 tells us that one of God's names is "Jealous": "Do not worship any other god, for the LORD, whose name is Jealous, is a jealous God."

Not only did God feel jealous when the Israelites gave their hearts to idols, but he directed that energy to draw his people back to himself. Through Jesus' death, he made a way to adopt new children and lavished his love upon them to remind his first children (the children of Israel) of his goodness. His motivation wasn't to hurt the Israelites. He wanted to show them what they were missing so they would return to him (Rom. 11:11). Just as God harnessed the power of his jealousy, so you can put your jealousy to work for a higher purpose.

It's important, therefore, to distinguish envy from jealousy—and the issues underlying these feelings. For example, envy may reflect a crisis of faith, a low self-image, or an insidious fear of failure and loss. When befriended it can become deep respect and admiration for another person.

Likewise, getting to know your jealousy will benefit your internal family. Are your jealous feelings coming from an exiled insecurity or from a genuine desire to protect something you love?

If you're not certain, follow the Five Steps to find out. Honor your longings and redirect your unmet desire. Take a You-Turn to befriend these powerful feelings and turn them into your greatest allies.

> ## Caution: Entitlement Mentality at Work!
>
> Parts of you may believe you deserve the things you desire and you're owed whatever you want: *I deserve to have a wonderful spouse; I deserve to have accomplished children; or I deserve to have success.* As you listen to your envy and invite Jesus to be near it, gently remind it of what you know in your heart to be true: that you're not entitled to anything, and that he gave you every good thing in your life as a generous gift. Then harness envy's energy, reshape your dreams in partnership with God—and watch his divine plan unfold.

THE CAUSE OF ENVY: UNMET DESIRE

What causes your envy? We've discussed that the main cause is a tender, unmet desire that envy attempts to protect. Facing your envy brings you into contact with your deepest desires hiding beneath it. These desires are a double-edged sword: They can remind you of missed opportunities, leading you down a path of regret. They can also drive you to pursue meaningful passions or connection with others and greater fulfillment in your life.

For example, when I, Alison, was in graduate school, I found myself envying a woman I worked for. I didn't want to envy this lovely woman who had been nothing but kind to me. I hated feeling that way. But as I faced my envy, I became aware of unacknowledged longings inside my soul. And, over time, I began to realign parts of my soul in support of pursuing what had been a hidden desire. I shifted from envying her to recognizing she had much to teach me.

Desire can be painful, even dangerous. To open yourself to desire means becoming vulnerable to loss and regret. No wonder you try to distance your desire and settle for envy. But desire can also drive you to build an abundant life. Without it, who would want to get out of bed in the morning? If you want to be whole, open your heart to your desire and lead it gently before God.

Once when I, Kim, was a kid at summer camp, I wrote home to my mom that I missed her and was lonely. I wanted to have friends, but when I first arrived at camp I didn't. I would check off each passing day on my calendar, waiting until I could see her again. She wrote me back with good advice: find another camper who also seems homesick and ask her to do something fun. Soon after, I found myself on our cabin rooftop with new friends and our fun counselor, who was letting us have contraband chewing gum for one special night. Gazing at the stars and listening to country music on the radio together, I remember thinking, *The party's going on right here!*

God doesn't promise to give you everything you want, and yet he wants you to be satisfied. In fact, he gives you longings so he can ultimately fulfill them. When you surrender your dreams to him, the sting of unfulfilled desire subsides. He works gently in your heart to honor your loss and help you design new dreams. With his Spirit leading your soul, you'll find yourself journeying from the angst of isolation to purposeful connection. IFS founder Richard Schwartz paints a hopeful picture with these words: "Think of what your life might be like if all the energy you spent, for example, angrily stewing about what others have done to you, or obsessively daydreaming about your missing soulmate, were available to you in the present moment and were channeled toward fully enjoying whatever you are doing now."[5]

CREATE THE LIFE OF YOUR DREAMS

In one of his most famous sermons, C. S. Lewis vividly illustrated the value of desire. He upended the misconception that trusting God with desires leads to a grim, unfulfilling life. Lewis suggested, instead, that God wants to fulfill our desires. On June 8, 1941, in a sermon titled "The Weight of Glory," he taught:

> We are told to deny ourselves and to take up our crosses in order that we may follow Christ; and nearly every description of what we shall ultimately find if we do so contains an appeal to desire. . . . It would seem that Our Lord finds our desires not too strong, but too weak. We are half-hearted creatures, fooling about with drink and sex and ambition when infinite joy is offered us, like an ignorant child who wants to go on making mud pies in a slum because he cannot imagine what is meant by the offer of a holiday at the sea. We are far too easily pleased.[6]

If a longing part of you wanders off like a prodigal child and ends up playing in the mud, become the capable leader it desperately needs. Embrace your desire and then lead it with love. Invite Jesus to be with it. Hand over your burdens of fear and regret, and receive new gifts—and new dreams—from him, the most precious of which is the gift of his presence.

PUT ENVY AND DESIRE TO WORK FOR YOUR HIGHEST GOOD

Your envy can notify you of unmet desire, signaling you to examine what's missing in your life. Envy and desire can become the dreamers in your internal family. How can you develop the qualities you wish you had? Let your envy and desire motivate you to design your life thoughtfully and make your own creative contribution to the world.

Facing desire is not for the faint of heart. But take courage, because God can fulfill your desires and longings by giving you the good things he wants for you. It's amazing what happens when we give our dreams to him.

Chapter 13

BOUNDARIES WITH GUILT AND SHAME

*To embrace and love who we are, we have
to reclaim and reconnect with the parts of
ourselves we've orphaned over the years.*
—Brené Brown, *Rising Strong: The Reckoning.
The Rumble. The Revolution.*

No one who hopes in you will ever be put to shame.
—Psalm 25:3

guilt
gĭlt
noun
"a painful emotion experienced when one believes one's
actions or thoughts have violated a moral or personal
standard"[1]

shame
shām/
noun

"a painful emotion caused by the belief that one is, or is perceived by others to be, inferior or unworthy of affection or respect because of one's actions, thoughts, circumstances, or experiences"[2]

WHAT IF YOU could trade your shame for a life of joy and creativity? Unburdening your shame is more possible than you ever thought. Read on to discover how.

In the garden, Adam and Eve were unashamed (Gen. 2:25). But the dawn of sin brought the dawn of shame. And to this day, each person has to face this painful emotion. The burden of shame comes from evil, from others, and from your inner critic. Evil wants to stifle the freedom that comes with knowing you're loved. People hurt you with their actions, cutting remarks, dismissive eye rolls, and furrowed brows. And your shaming protectors unwittingly take the bait, increasing condemnation and the threat of isolation.

How do you move from a life of self-sabotaging shame and discover the peace that comes from accepting yourself—with your human limitations as well as your God-given potential? In this chapter, we'll explore how to make the crucial transition to a life of goodness, creativity, and authentic connection. You can redirect your misguided inner critic. You can befriend the weary parts of your soul carrying burdens of guilt and shame. So step out of the stronghold and receive the treasures that Jesus, the lover of your soul, longs to pour into your life.

On which side of this line do you tend to live your life?

Self-Condemnation

_____

Self-Acceptance

JULIE TAKES A YOU-TURN WHEN SHE FEELS SHAME

"I hurt so much I can barely breathe," Julie said, wringing her hands. "The criticism feels like a knife to my heart. No matter how hard I try to catch up at work, I only fall further behind. I'm such a failure."

Julie came to see me, Alison, because she needed help navigating a tense relationship with her supervisor, Jeff. He was accusing Julie of not contributing her fair share on an important project. Julie's husband was leaving her for another woman, and her son was moving back in after losing his job. When Julie explained why she was falling behind, her supervisor became even more accusatory, calling her "unreliable" and complaining about how much overtime he had worked to compensate for her performance gap.

Bad dreams awakened Julie at night. Unable to get back to sleep, she would lie awake for hours rehearsing her troubles, then drag herself to work the next day, counting the minutes until she could leave. Feeling paralyzed emotionally, Julie fantasized about escaping her pain: *It would be easier if I didn't exist*, she caught herself thinking. But these mortifying thoughts further increased her sense of worthlessness.

As I talked with Julie, I could tell she was working hard to see the situation objectively. She understood her supervisor's frustration about picking up the slack at work—slack created by Julie's life crisis. But where was Jeff's compassion? "I've been a dependable employee for years. Now I'm going through one of the most painful trials in my life," she cried, "and all Jeff can do is criticize me and demand I work harder." No matter how hard Julie tried to stay positive, Jeff's accusing words had taken root in her soul.

Focus and Befriend

As we continued our session, I asked Julie if she could picture her shame. She closed her eyes and, engaging her prayerful imagination, said that it was as if an arrow had pierced straight through her heart. As she focused on this image, I asked Julie how she felt toward it. She replied that she noticed a second, critical part of herself . . . a part that was shooting the arrows. This inner critic seemed to have picked up Jeff's arrows and was using them to shame her by saying, *You're a useless waste of space.*

"I've tried telling myself that Jeff is a heartless jerk," Julie said. "But shooting the arrow back at him doesn't help—it makes me feel worse. I guess this critical part of me would rather I feel the shame."

I asked Julie if mentally rehearsing Jeff's harsh messages was helping. She said no but that her inner critic didn't know what else to do. As she focused on this shaming part with curiosity, however, it began to soften and step back.

"I feel calmer," Julie said, indicating that her Spirit-led self was taking the lead.

Invite and Unburden

I asked Julie if she wanted to invite Jesus to draw near, trusting that he knew what to do with her pain.

Julie felt tears welling back up in her eyes. "Yes," she said. "When I heard you say that Jesus might be able to help me find another way, I saw an image of a hurting baby. This younger part of me needs to know that someone wants to be with her. She feels so useless. She's looking around for Jesus because she knows he can take this feeling away. Now he's holding her in his arms and telling her she's important—that he wants to be with her."

"Does this part of you need anything from him?" I asked.

"His peace," Julie said softly. "She is finally feeling his peace."

Summary of Julie's You-Turn

When Julie *focused* on, *befriended*, and *invited* Jesus to draw near to her shaming inner critic, then she was able to find the exile it protected—the source of her pain. She sought Jesus' help to care for this young part of her soul, which she prayerfully imagined as a baby feeling useless and alone. She *unburdened* and became stronger internally as she sensed Jesus tenderly reassuring her vulnerable exile. No longer shaming herself or carrying the burden of feeling "useless," Julie could formulate a plan to advocate for herself. She requested a leave of absence so she could take more time to heal—evidence that she had integrated her hardworking protector constructively into her internal family.

UNDERSTANDING SHAME

As demonstrated in Julie's story, shame is a persistent emotional burden that a tender exile carries when believing the hurtful messages of a shaming inner critic: *you don't have what it takes; you're bad and not worthy of love.* Parts that carry this burden of shame believe that you don't matter or belong. All-or-nothing, black-or-white thinkers, they repeat dreary refrains like broken records. You might try to forget the past and move on. The pain won't relent, though, and you feel stuck and overwhelmed. Carrying a burden of shame erodes your sense of self-respect over time, crippling your soul and stifling your joy.

What if both of these parts—your shaming inner critic and the exile carrying the burden of shame—could become your allies? Given adequate time and attention, they can. The healing process begins with focusing gently on these parts and listening to them. Appreciate both your inner critic and your burdened exile for their hard work and get to know them better. Help them find rest in the presence of your Spirit-led self. Here's an example of this process from my, Kim's, life.

LESSONS FROM LIMITATIONS

Once, when I was talking with some friends about learning from limitations, I found myself sharing about a dark valley I had been through. The next morning, I woke up "hung over" with shame, as Brené Brown describes. I wanted to crawl out of my skin. My chest was clenched, and I felt sick to my stomach. Engulfed in a tsunami of regret, I wondered, *Will those people ever talk to me again? Was I too much for them? Why did I have to go and ruin everything?* And then I asked myself, *How do I make this pain go away?* Thankfully, I remembered: *Oh yes, I can take a You-Turn!*

I focused my attention on the feeling and at the same time became aware of an irate voice in my mind—a voice that was absolutely furious with me. I could imagine this critical part of myself hurling insults and profanities. *Wow,* I thought. *I'm glad no one can hear what I'm thinking!*

I get you, I responded from my Spirit-led self, and immediately my inner critic softened. *This stuff works,* I thought, smiling.

I continued listening intentionally, from my Spirit-led self, and the shame feelings subsided. *Focusing* and *befriending* helped me get some relief. *What's next?* I thought, *Oh yeah—invite.* And so, I invited Jesus to draw near this exhausted inner critic. Jesus said, *I love you. I'm so proud of you. You have so much to give.* Oh, how I love Jesus. He is so good!

My angry critic then handed over its rage to Jesus, and my exile handed over its sense of shame to him too.

In the presence of Jesus and my Spirit-led self, my critic backed off from berating me. What remained was curiosity: *Did*

I share appropriately? Should I not have shared about my painful experience?

And because everyone can benefit from consulting with a personal "boundaries committee," I called Alison to see whether she thought my sharing had been helpful. "Absolutely, it was helpful," she said. I beamed in response, partly because I had shared appropriately, and partly because I had coached myself through a successful You-Turn. I had cared for the hurting part of myself and eased the pressure on my friend to be my first responder. And I was grateful for her affirmation of what I had already heard from God.

Benefits, Dangers, Needs, and Fears

Consider the benefits, dangers, needs, and fears associated with shame.

Benefits

Shame can indicate that something in your life needs to change. The feeling of shame can:

- lead you to parts of yourself that need your attention
- signal when you're overestimating your own power
- be an invitation to step out in courage and creativity
- alert you to emotional danger
- motivate you to discover your true identity

Dangers

Shame *will* show up. The question is, when, where, and how? Unaddressed shame surfaces in unhealthy ways, leading to:

- the feeling that you aren't good enough and something is inherently wrong with you
- interruption of your creative process and a hesitation to take risks

- defensiveness, fear of rejection, and the tendency to withdraw from others
- lying, blaming, manipulating, and people-pleasing
- internal unrest or chaos, including suicidal thoughts

Needs

Perhaps more than any other emotion, the part of your soul carrying shame wants your attention and needs to:

- learn to be vulnerable and experience the compassion of your Spirit-led self
- learn a new perspective—that you don't have to beat yourself up
- let Jesus mend the injury that caused your shame
- trust you to choose emotionally safe people with whom you can speak carefully on its behalf (and not share with people who may reinjure you or shame you even more)
- practice hearing God's voice of truth and love

Fears

Like all other parts of your soul, the part of you carrying your shame wants to help you—even though its methods may be misguided. Learn why it resists letting your Spirit-led self take the lead. Common examples of those fears are:

- *I'll be proved a fool.*
- *I'll be exposed as a fraud.*
- *I'll be cut off, shut out, rejected, and alone.*

When you notice the feeling of shame in your own life, take a You-Turn and focus on this burdened part of your soul that needs your attention. If it's too close to you, listen and show up for it. As you do, it will take a step back. Then, as the part of you carrying shame develops trust in your Spirit-led self, it can help you develop a new understanding of who you are.

PLAYERS IN THE SHAME GAME

In addition to your shaming inner critic, you might experience an overly guilty conscience or be perfectionistic. However a protector part shows up for you, focus on it, befriend it, and get to know the burdened part it protects so that you can be set free. Let's look more closely now at these managers that play the tricky game of shame.

The Shaming Inner Critic

In a misguided effort to help you improve, your shaming inner critic reminds you of all the ways you don't measure up. In response, an exile harbors this false message. But your Spirit-led self knows better and can set the record straight.

Often, as with Julie, the accusing words or critical attitudes of another person set this shaming inner critic on its course. The accusations might be personal and linked to a current conflict. Or they might be rooted in words that were spoken—or left unspoken—by a caregiver or authority figure long ago.

Either way, the accusing words, insinuations, or critical attitudes rouse your shaming inner critic. Thinking it's helping, your critic berates you, and an exile weighed down with the burden of shame pays the price. We've found that what helps is to *focus* on it, *befriend* it, *invite* Jesus to draw near, and *unburden* it. Let it take in the truth that God loves you just as you are. Then *integrate* this newly transformed critic into your internal family and put it to work reminding you of God's powerful love.

Seek to understand a shaming inner critic, and invariably you'll encounter an exile that carries a burden as a result. This younger part might be holding on to painful memories of experiences that left you feeling rejected or isolated. Perhaps you were abused or exposed to violence as a child. Or maybe you grew up around addiction or mental illness or were embarrassed by having made a mistake. Parts can carry these experiences into the present. Sometimes present-day struggles make us susceptible to feeling shame. For example, Julie's shaming inner critic berated her for falling behind at work. No matter its origin, the burden of shame stifles your joy and keeps you from letting your light shine.

To work with an exile carrying shame, first focus on it from your Spirit-led self. You may experience it as an overwhelming feeling of wanting to hide or crawl out of your skin. Or you may notice it as a thought that you're not good enough or you're a terrible person. Stay present with the exile carrying this burden until you become curious about it and compassionate toward it. Then invite Jesus to be near. The burden of shame doesn't stand a chance in the power of God's presence. "God is kind, but he's not soft. In kindness, he takes us firmly by the hand and leads us into a radical life-change" (Rom. 2:4 MSG).

Julie's ashamed exile was overwhelming her and hadn't received the care it needed. So when Jeff started criticizing her at work, the feeling of shame increased exponentially. Though Jeff's words were not caring, God eventually used them for good in Julie's life. Through this experience, Julie strengthened her sense of her own identity and intrinsic value in God's sight. She grew in her ability to advocate for herself and to ask for what she needed. As she faced her pain, she learned that talking about her wounds and losses was necessary and helpful. And she began to understand that, rather than striving for perfection, her vulnerabilities made her approachable, relatable, and even more beautiful.

A Guilty Conscience

In areas of temptation, your guilty conscience fights like a warrior. This valiant part battles with other parts of your soul to do the right thing. Without it your firefighters, for example, might destroy your life by derailing you with endless, destructive, "feel-good" behavior. Listen to this part of you that does the hard work of keeping you on the road that leads to life—it can serve as an important adviser.

King David was *too far* from his guilt when he called for Bathsheba and plotted to kill her husband. Likewise, he was too far from his guilt when he failed to discipline his rebellious sons, ultimately contributing to their corruption and even, in some cases, to their death. Later he demonstrated that he had come to value his guilt when he confessed in Psalm 51, "I have sinned." His story is a cautionary tale.

Sometimes guilt can get *too close* and become extreme. In this case, your conscience becomes a guilt-tripper—harping on you for making a mistake. When guilt overtakes you, even asking forgiveness and making amends won't alleviate your sense of failure. Whereas a guilty part at a healthy distance leads to confession, repentance, and renewal, guilt that's too close weighs down an exiled part of your soul. It nags you for doing something wrong—even when you didn't. It doesn't want you to accept your human limitations and the grief you might need to feel. And it may try to convince you of the lie that, without its constant reminders about all the ways you fall short, God won't love you. But Jesus did too much on the cross for that message to be true.

As you get to know your guilt, you may find that you indeed have something to confess. Or you may find that you have a burden of false guilt. In this case, it may be that you are considering yourself to be more powerful than you are. Rest in the knowledge that he is in control.

A Perfectionistic Part

On a quest for love, significance, and security, perfectionistic parts work tirelessly to prove your worth.[3] For example, my,

Alison's, mom loves to recount how her perfectionism met its match in my dad during their early years of marriage. Shortly after his return from Vietnam, they returned to his hometown and rented their first home together. Having not had the best of childhoods, my mom feared not being able to create a happy family. Her perfectionistic manager defined domestic happiness as meticulous housekeeping, so she threw herself into perfecting their tiny rental.

Each day, she vacuumed thoroughly, ensuring that fresh vacuum-cleaner tracks appeared on the carpet. One night a few weeks into their marriage, my mom greeted my dad at the door and politely requested that he walk around the tracks on the freshly vacuumed carpet. My dad declined her request, replying that he planned to *live* in their house.

In this moment of reckoning, my mother's perfectionistic manager bumped up against a part of my father that had a different perspective on what makes a happy home. And thankfully, her love for my dad helped her manager part relax and adjust its strategy. The simple decision to cede her perfect vacuum tracks set her—and their life together—off on a new path. Throughout my parents' nearly fifty years of marriage, they've created what Madeleine L'Engle calls a "two-part invention"—a partnership that harmonizes two interdependent parts like two melodies.[4] My mom leads her perfectionistic part to create a warm home, brimming with hospitality, and my dad's gregarious, happy-go-lucky part helps them fill the house with a joyful community of family, neighbors, and friends.

If you have a perfectionistic part, understand that it's trying to keep you from feelings of shame. As was the case with my, Alison's, mom, your perfectionistic part may have developed as you grew up in your family of origin: Perhaps you received messages that you needed to perform in order to be accepted and loved. Or maybe you felt that all your parents' hopes and dreams were pinned on you. Perhaps you experienced social pressure or grew up in a family with secrets about alcoholism, drug addiction,

191

or abuse. Now that you're an adult, your inner perfectionist may be working overtime to disprove the message that you are defined by your past. It might believe shaming messages, such as, *If I can do enough perfectly, my pain will go away.*

In her popular TED talk, "The Power of Vulnerability," Brené Brown teaches that wholehearted people have the courage to reveal their imperfections to others—and to themselves. They're willing to let go of who they should be in order to be who they are.[5] *Coeur*, from which we get our English word *courage*, means "heart" in Latin. It takes courage to tell the authentic story of who you are.

If you struggle with an inner critic, an overly guilty conscience, or a perfectionistic part, *focus*, *befriend*, and *invite* Jesus to draw near. These well-meaning protectors have been working for a long time and could use some well-deserved rest.

REWRITING YOUR NARRATIVE

The sense of being bad drives parts from one another inside your soul and causes you to isolate from other people too. Psychiatrist and author of the powerful book *The Soul of Shame*, Curt Thompson wrote that much of shame's power "lies in its ability to isolate, both within and between minds."[6] Isolation leads to anguish and stifles your creativity.

But the burden of shame, the belief that you are bad, could not be further from the truth. The Holy Spirit beckons you to reconnect and believe that you are loved just as you are. How are you making sense of what you have experienced? Are you letting the past send parts of yourself into hiding and isolate you from others? Respond to shame, Thompson says, by retelling your personal story in light of the biblical story that proves how much God loves you.[7]

How do you go about rewriting the narrative believed by the part of you carrying the burden of shame? Get to know this part of yourself. Think of how Jesus went into the desert where he could face the devil head-on, Thompson suggests. Likewise, notice the refrain being repeated again and again by the part of your soul believing evil's lie. Thompson also encourages keeping a shame inventory (including writing down how many times a day you feel shame) to interrupt shaming neuropathways and "to pay attention to what you're paying attention to."[8] Then write a new story in light of the fact that God cherishes you. Instead of carrying the belief *I don't matter*, tell yourself the truth: *I can be real because I belong to him*. If you practice believing that new narrative, the hurting parts of your internal family will regain trust in your Spirit-led self. You'll integrate your inner critic and exile into a team of (former) rivals.

UNBURDENING SHAME

The part of you that once spoke shame, when transformed in the presence of your Spirit-led self, will become an advocate of transparency. It will remind you of the value in letting down your guard and accepting your human limitations. Once debilitating you, the part of you that understands the burden of shame will now create a welcoming environment for your internal family and for others. And the more resilient you become, the more you will invite others into that experience of authenticity.

> Burdens of shame do not define you. Whereas these lies say you are unimportant, God says you are decidedly well-known *and* deeply loved. And you can be real because you are his.

Burdens of shame do not define you. Whereas these lies say you are unimportant, God says you are decidedly well-known *and* deeply loved. And you can be real because you are his. You are the light of the world—and shame has no place in the light.

Chapter 14

BOUNDARIES WITH CHALLENGING PARTS OF OTHERS

Whether or not you realize the full potential of this
[relationship] vision depends not on your ability to
attract the perfect mate, but on your willingness to
acquire knowledge about hidden parts of yourself.

—Harville Hendrix, *Getting the Love You Want*

If we could read the secret history of our enemies,
we should find in each man's life sorrow and
suffering enough to disarm all hostility.

—Henry Wadsworth Longfellow

"Ted said he doesn't love me anymore," said the urgent text from my friend Isabel. I, Kim, knew her marriage was in trouble, but this message caught me off guard. As I stood in my kitchen flipping breakfast pancakes, Isabel's life flashed before my eyes. *It's her second marriage,* I thought to myself, *and now it's over!*

Overwhelmed with sadness at the thought of my friend's

pain, I paused to take a You-Turn to calm the part of me that was feeling distraught. That's when it hit me: Ted was speaking from a *part* of himself.

Fortunately, Isabel had been learning about Spirit-led self-leadership. She had also been learning about the different parts of the soul. So I felt confident she would respond well to my encouragement not to react to words that clearly were coming from a protective, but no doubt well-meaning, part of Ted. Isabel and I both knew he loved her in his heart of hearts and wanted their marriage to work.

"Do you think a *part* of Ted might be struggling?" I texted back.

"Now that you mention it, I do," came Isabel's reply.

Later Isabel told me that the realization that Ted had been speaking from a struggling part of himself "changed everything." Whereas she had initially felt devastated, reframing Ted's words brought her perspective and calmed her heart. As a result, Isabel didn't catastrophize the situation. And together she and Ted charted a course out of dangerous waters.

Earlier in my life, I might have replied to Isabel's SOS signal with a response like, "How awful! I can't believe he would say that to you!" Or "You deserve to be treated better than that!" But these responses, though well-intentioned, could have magnified my friend's despair and contributed to her conflict. I'm grateful I'm learning a better way—and that my critical part is learning to become a *parts detective.*

TRANSFORMING YOUR CRITIC INTO A PARTS DETECTIVE

A well-developed internal parts detective identifies when someone is speaking or behaving from a hijacking protector or an overwhelming exile—when anger, fear, or some other emotion has eclipsed that person's Spirit-led self. Instead of wrangling with that part, your internal parts detective prompts you to get curious about it: *I wonder why she's acting that way.* Or *I wonder what pain he's feeling underneath his anger.* You can assist others who are hurting by de-escalating tense situations, setting external boundaries, and creating opportunities for deeper connection.

Turning your well-meaning critic into a parts detective doesn't mean you're authorized to recklessly point out when someone else has been taken over by a rebellious part. Instead, it means growing in your understanding that a well-meaning part may be instigating someone's hurtful behavior. When you find someone to be difficult, put your parts detective to work wisely and discreetly. Don't misuse your insights, but seek to grow in understanding.

Having devoted the preceding chapters to developing healthy boundaries on the *inside,* in this final chapter, we'll examine how these internal boundaries can help you establish healthy boundaries with others. Specifically, let's consider how to:

- respond to others in need
- resolve conflicts
- love others who have what we call "parts in process"
- create deeper connection and more satisfying relationships
- maintain healthy distance from unsafe parts of other people

Responding to Others in Need

We want to care well for others. Unfortunately, our loved ones' struggles often trigger our own troubling emotions, making it difficult to be of real help. How do you respond when someone shares a problem with you?

When someone shares a need or frustration, the following four types of responses are common but are not always most helpful. Do you recognize your own go-to method here?

1. **Agreement.** You join in with the person and blame someone else for the problem: *"I can't believe she did that to you!"*
2. **Pep Talk.** You encourage the person to recognize that she doesn't really need to feel this way: *"But you're such a great person! Don't let it get you down."*
3. **Minimizing.** You try to downplay the problem—to avoid facing a painful reality: *"At least it's not worse!"*
4. **Fixing.** You offer a quick fix to a complicated problem: *"You should just stop thinking about it!"*

There's a time and a place for agreeing, pep talks, minimizing, and fixing—and we can do more. As our Spirit-led self leads, we can become "Sabbath for one another."[1] To become a friend whose presence invites rest and reflection, practice taking a You-Turn, and notice what happens inside of *you* when someone comes to you in need.

As you cultivate Spirit-led self-leadership, you'll be better equipped to respond constructively to friends and loved ones. The following ideas may also help you create opportunities for deeper connection the next time someone shares a problem or a painful feeling with you:

- Acknowledge the other person's hurting part by asking, "Have you considered that this part of you exists for a reason and has good intentions? How might it be trying to help you?"
- Ask the person how she feels *toward* the part that is hurting. In doing so, you might help her identify an inner critic or an exiled fear. Encouraging her to get to know her own protectors will help her take a You-Turn.
- Remind her that the person who has hurt her probably is behaving from a part too. She doesn't have to like that part,

but the understanding will help her realize there's more to this offending person than the part that hurt her.

• Offer to pray for the part of her that's suffering. And offer to pray for the part of the person who hurt her.

"Blessed are the peacemakers," Jesus said in the Sermon on the Mount (Matt. 5:9). As you live increasingly from your Spirit-led self, you'll become an instrument of peace and help your friends become peacemakers too.

Resolving Conflict: The Power of Curiosity and Compassion

Let's move now from responding to people in need to resolving difficult interpersonal conflicts. What if you are the one with a painful relationship issue? In difficult situations, maintaining intimacy—the experience of close connection—involves getting *curious* about your own vulnerabilities and the ways you seek to protect yourself. And it involves learning to share constructively on behalf of those exiles and protectors. (See "Speaking on Behalf of a Part, Rather Than from It," in chapter 4.) Resolving conflict also involves turning your well-meaning critic of others into a parts detective, becoming adept at discerning the vulnerabilities of the ones you love, and thus learning to view them with compassion.

Whereas helplessness leads to depression, moving into a place of agency and self-advocacy brings joy—when you're living by the Spirit. So, prayerfully seek God's help for the creative courage to stand up for this part of yourself, even if standing up means deciding to love and pray for the other person *from a comfortable distance.*

Here is an example of how I, Kim, learned to resolve conflict.

It was a busy season in our marriage. My husband, Ken, was writing under a tight deadline, and I was preparing to lead a soul-care retreat. While we focused on these commitments, our stack of unopened mail grew higher and higher. On my way to and from the coffeemaker each day, I eyed it with growing aggravation. A part of me insisted that someone take action—I couldn't focus on my retreat preparation until this administrative mission had been accomplished. The mail was cluttering our kitchen and my mind. And to make matters worse, Ken didn't seem troubled at all.

After much stewing, my reformer part sought out an opportunity to settle the matter and waited for the right moment.

Sure enough, one morning Ken smiled kindly and said, "Your birthday's coming up, and I'm wondering what you would like this year."

"I'd like you to help me with the mail for one hour," I instantly replied.

From the bewildered look on his face, I could see that a part of Ken wasn't at all enthused by my idea for a birthday present.

"How about I take you out for a romantic dinner?" he responded cautiously.

And just like that, there was tension between us. Thankfully, within a few hours, my Spirit-led self prompted me to take a You-Turn.

First, I realized a part of me was anxious about the growing pile of mail that wasn't magically disappearing. I focused on this worried reformer part and came to appreciate its fear that Ken and I might overlook some important letter or bill. Befriending my worry, I invited Jesus to draw near. I handed over to him my fear and received peace in exchange. Then I recruited this peaceful part to advise me about how to speak with Ken moving forward. As a result of my You-Turn, I was able to speak on behalf of my fear with intentionality instead of being reactive.

The next evening, I waited in the kitchen for Ken to come home from work. When he walked in the door, he held open his arms for a hug. "Honey," I said, "I'm sorry. I love you and know you love me. And a part of me is feeling anxious that some things aren't getting done."

Once he understood that I was feeling anxious, we were able to conquer the mountain of mail together! We felt more connected to each other and, from that place, were able to clarify our respective responsibilities at home.

This experience reminded me that, when problem-solving, it's crucial to develop emotional awareness and share new discoveries with the ones I love. Speaking on behalf of my worried reformer part freed us to enjoy working together—and to be reminded all over again that we make a great team!

One useful habit to develop with a close friend or spouse is simply to agree that when one of you feels anxiety, or any other challenging emotion, you'll say, "Just a moment, please. I'm taking a You-Turn." This simple practice works well for Ken and me. As a result, instead of experiencing one another's reaction with the burden of having to figure out what it's about and how to deal with it, we engage in our own process of reflection. Then we can speak more clearly and lovingly to one another.

As you gain perspective about a part that is either too close to or too far from your Spirit-led self, such as one carrying anger, grief, or insecurities, you'll be able to connect more genuinely with that emotion or belief. As a result of the good communication that forms internally, you'll find you communicate more effectively with others too. And effective communication is just one of the many ways that caring for your soul helps you spread the love of Christ to those around you.

So, to review, developing healthy boundaries during conflict involves:

- differentiating from your own unruly emotion
- connecting (or reconnecting) from your Spirit-led self

with this emotion, forming a healthier, stronger internal attachment

- communicating your feelings and requests lovingly to others

Loving Others in Process

Every single one of us is a masterpiece. And at the same time, you might say we all have *parts in process*. So we can expect difficulties to arise in even the healthiest of relationships. For example, your spouse may have made a career decision that's going to create hardship for you. Or your adult child may not make time for you. Perhaps your best friend boasts about the opportunity of a lifetime and you feel left behind. Accessing the creativity and patience of your Spirit-led self often starts when your parts detective alerts you that your loved one's annoying habit or hurtful behavior is the action of a well-meaning *part*. Equipped with this awareness, develop strategies to engage with the part of the other person in more effective ways.

To care well for troubled parts of your own soul, and the struggling parts of those you love, first consider your expectations. Doing so is important because, when it comes to relationships, as the saying goes, "It takes two." You might have an entitled or demanding part that feels you're owed perfect understanding and care. In this case, your expectations are too high. Or you might have an ostrich part wanting to stick its head in the sand, hoping the problem will magically vanish! In this case, your expectations—of others, yourself, the situation, or *all three*—are too low.

Where are you on this spectrum between being demanding and being diminished? Put a mark on the graph below to indicate your answer:

Diminished————Healthy Expectations————Demanding
I don't deserve anything.   *I deserve perfection.*

When you're leading from your Spirit-led self and have healthy expectations of loved ones, you won't be harsh, but loving when setting boundaries with others. If your sibling tends to pick a fight when he's tired or stressed, for example, notice that part of him, get curious about it, and don't engage until you've had a chance to take a You-Turn. If he's someone with whom you can talk about the pattern, great. If not, be strategic about when and how you spend time with him. Noticing your own reactions—and those of others—allows you to advocate for tender parts of yourself, at times without saying a word. And if you wait patiently for the right time and way to bring up your frustration, you'll maximize your opportunity for a successful conversation.

Think of genuine affirmations you can give to the hardworking, albeit challenging, part of a loved one that's still in process. Try validating that part of her for how well it fulfills its role. (It works!) For example, consider complimenting your mother-in-law when she offers you well-meaning but uninvited child-rearing advice: "You raised a man who is a great husband. I appreciate what a wonderful mother you are." Instead of harboring resentment, get curious and practice acknowledging the good intention beneath her sometimes overly involved part. In *The Gifts of Imperfection*, Brené Brown wrote, "When we are kind to ourselves, we create a reservoir of compassion that we can extend to others."[2]

How Brain Science Improves Intimacy: The Wisdom of Emotional Connection

When you take a You-Turn and differentiate from parts of your soul, naming them and connecting with them in a loving way, you lay the groundwork for developing healthy boundaries in your relationships with others. The integrated model for doing so, presented in this book, has a strong foundation in psychology and neuroscience. Since the 1970s, much has been learned about the subject of boundaries. Murray Bowen, the first psychologist to apply the scientific term *differentiation* to human relationships, explained the difference between the "thinking" brain and the "emotional" brain. He called this separation within the human soul *differentiation* as well.

Bowen viewed emotions as the "out of control," or immature, realm of the psyche. He posited that the cerebral cortex (the "thinking" brain) should have dominance over the brain's "primitive" limbic region, which controls basic emotions. He believed in becoming more grounded in logical functions while controlling and suppressing more primal emotions. At the time, the world's leading psychologists considered rationality superior to emotionality—with the former thought to be more mature and evolved.

Recent findings from neuroscience have taught us, however, that emotions play a valuable role in processing any situation. We now know that resolving conflict and achieving true connection requires working with emotions as well. We have a better understanding of how the brain processes emotion. We also know more about how *internal* differentiation (by which we mean parts of ourselves relating to one another in healthy ways) influences *interpersonal* attachments. In other words, scientific evidence tells us that high emotional intelligence, or having a deep understanding about one's own emotions, improves relationships with others too.

Likewise, John and Julie Gottman's research has shown that if we don't involve our emotions during conflict resolution, problems don't get solved. Both emotion and reason are found in the brain's "thinking" cerebral cortex region. Connecting with one's own emotions must accompany the process of developing healthy boundaries with others.

Respected interpersonal neurobiologist Dan Siegel also explained the importance of integrating emotion when problem-solving and extending care to others. He shared, for example, in his fascinating book *Mindsight*, "Naming an affect [an observable sign of emotion] soothes limbic firing. Sometimes we need to 'name it to tame it'. . . . The key is to link left and right."[3] He noted that the left brain correlates with what Bowen called the "thinking" brain and the right brain with the "emotional" brain. Conflicting emotions can create a sense of uncertainty. When the left brain names what the right brain is experiencing, however, you are better equipped to tolerate the ambiguity of emotion. This process of bringing together different and sometimes competing parts of yourself is a key to mental health.

Similarly, in his book *Anatomy of the Soul*, Christian psychiatrist Curt Thompson described our tendency to *disintegrate* internally, whereas sharing our emotions leads us to greater intimacy: "The mind, when left to its own volition, tends to disconnect. It often conspires to hide the truth (the depth of our emotion, memory, and relational patterns, as well as the reality of a God who loves us beyond belief) from ourselves and others." He went on to say, "We are more interested in knowing right from wrong (a dominantly left-brain hemisphere function used to cope with fear and shame) than knowing God, which requires the integration of all parts of the brain." Our quest to be "right"—a cognitive activity—can actually keep us from deep connection and a *holistic* knowledge of God and others.[4]

As you care for hurting parts of yourself, you'll be working in this holistic space, incorporating both emotion and cognition. Doing so will empower you to differentiate from the parts of your soul with unhelpful thoughts or feelings, and to connect with those parts in a healthy way. Then you'll be able to reintegrate them with other parts of your internal family, bringing them together in harmony. As you learn the art and science of establishing healthy internal boundaries, you'll gain perspective about yourself and you'll begin to see others with better perspective too.

Maintaining Healthy Distance from Others' Unsafe Parts

Try as you may to "live at peace with everyone" (Rom. 12:18), what do you do when you determine you can't resolve a conflict because the person who hurt you has parts that are too unsafe? Your parts detective can alert you when you need to protect yourself from people who are unwilling or unable to exercise Spirit-led self-leadership with their angry, critical, or manipulative parts. If you've been hurt repeatedly by such a person, it's important to pay attention. And remember: this person is not "completely evil," as we sometimes hear, but a creation of God who is acting *from* (instead of *on behalf of*) entrenched, wayward, and yes, *well-meaning* parts.

It may be that this person, whether an acquaintance, friend, or family member, isn't going to change anytime soon. In this case, the hurting part of *you* needs your Spirit-led self to lead it with careful attention and discernment—in another direction. It's time to get some healthy distance.

But what about instances when propriety, manners, or a responsibility to participate in certain rituals, such as family gatherings or work-related activities, require you to be in this person's presence? To minimize further injury, be intentional about placing healthy limits on your interactions and developing wise strategies. For example, list off-limits topics of conversation. Then excuse yourself or change the subject if a hurtful topic is mentioned. As needed, make scripts to help you speak assertively. Assure the vulnerable part of your soul that you're going to minimize the time it will have to be present with this hurtful person, and assure it that you will set boundaries on its behalf. You may decide to deploy the "buddy system" and promise yourself never to be alone with this person. Each time you follow through on these commitments, you'll build trust within your internal family.

In addition, remind yourself that fighting with a deeply entrenched protective part of another person is a battle you'll lose every time, bruised and scarred from the fray. Anchoring yourself in this awareness will help you become more discerning and proceed with caution.

The next time you interact with this person, imagine the injured or vulnerable part of yourself in its own little "room" in your soul. Assure it that you have everything it needs for protection. If you have yielded your life to Christ, you have his Spirit inside of you. The psalmist said, "God, you are a shield around me, my glory and the lifter of my head" (Ps. 3:3, paraphrased). Promise your injured part that, if possible, you won't ask it to be in the presence of another person's critical, mean, or abusive behaviors. Let it know that when you feel endangered, you'll walk away. As you honor your commitments to this part of your soul, you'll learn to trust yourself—to have confidence in the clear, calm leadership of your Spirit-led self.

As you encounter unsafe parts of others, it is also possible that an angry, protective part of you might be present—a part that wants to get even or utter a scathing remark. Through your prayerful imagination, consider first giving this part a medal of honor for its faithful service. Then put it to work for you as your newly appointed boundaries adviser, alerting you to times when your "safety zone" has been violated. Let this adviser know that your Spirit-led self will take the lead.

In some cases, you may want to confront the other person. If you don't get the optimal response, befriend your discouraged part and help it find a new role in your internal family. Increasingly, your discouraged part will develop trust in your Spirit-led self's good judgment when handling confrontations.

Strength develops from the inside out—from a confidence that emanates from your Spirit-led self as you care for the parts of yourself in need—a confidence that is forged through trust and nuanced self-understanding. Take time to develop that kind of strength, and you will not be shaken.

GRACE FILLS IN THE GAPS

Thankfully, nothing can separate us from the love of God. Through his life, death, and resurrection, Jesus offers boundless forgiveness to everyone with a repentant heart. He forgives us and cleanses us when we confess our sin to him (1 John 1:9). And because God offers forgiveness to us in abundance, we, too, are called to forgive—ourselves *and* others.

In some cases, forgiving comes easily. At other times, it can be challenging, requiring an act of daily surrender. When wounds are deep, we may find it's necessary to forgive ourselves or another for the same offense repeatedly, as fresh layers of pain are exposed in our suffering hearts. In heaven we'll be able to "fully and finally forgive," notes theologian N. T. Wright.[5] Until then we can participate in expanding God's kingdom by working toward forgiveness.

To facilitate the forgiveness process, think of someone you're having trouble forgiving. With that person in mind, complete the following sentences:

1. The incident that I have trouble forgiving is . . .
2. One time I demonstrated even a little bit of the same behavior was when . . .
3. What hurt me most about the incident I'm having trouble forgiving was . . .
4. The core wound that it touched from my childhood was . . .
5. The unspoken understanding we had, which was broken, was . . .
6. The aspect of my character that contributed to the conflict is . . . (Note: This step doesn't apply if the injury occurred in childhood.)

7. What I know or imagine about this person that helps me make sense of why he behaved the way he did is . . .
8. The fears I have about letting go at this time are . . .
9. The reality of who I am is . . .
10. The good, bad, or "what might have been" that I'm ready to say goodbye to is . . .
11. The gifts I'm grateful to have gained from this painful experience are . . .
12. The next piece of work I need to do to continue the process of healing is . . .

A PARTING PRAYER FOR YOUR FUTURE SELF

As we've explored the steps of Spirit-led self-leadership throughout these pages, we're mindful that we're still on our own journeys toward wholeness. But we stay the course, confident that on this path we are becoming the people God created us to be. As Paul wrote, "I press on toward the goal for the prize of the upward call of God in Christ Jesus" (Phil. 3:14 NASB).

Because God offers forgiveness to us in abundance, we, too, are called to forgive—ourselves *and* others.

As you also "press on," take a moment now and imagine yourself as God sees you. What burdens are you laying down? What qualities are you taking in from the One who loves you most? Receive them in abundance now and share them generously with others.

Remember these truths from God's Word—unshakable realities that apply to every part of the life surrendered to him: You are adopted, accepted, called by name. You are hidden with Christ, chosen, forgiven, washed clean, and redeemed. You have been given the Spirit of God, strength, mercy, grace, and access to the Holy of Holies. You have been given the mind of Christ. You are complete in him, you are clothed with his righteousness, and you are secure in his love.[6]

You have tremendous capacity to encourage wholeness and abundant living in everyone around you. As you continue on this journey, we pray that you might know God's delight, great love, and pride in you. May God minister to you and give you freedom and joy, in this life and into eternity. May the power of God be at work in every part of you—the sanctimonious, the straying, and the suffering—that they may be found, befriended, and restored.

MAP OF THE SOUL

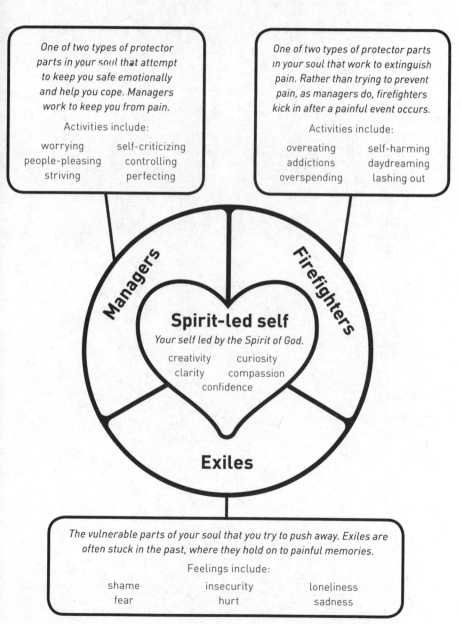

One of two types of protector parts in your soul that attempt to keep you safe emotionally and help you cope. Managers work to keep you from pain.

Activities include:

worrying   self-criticizing
people-pleasing   controlling
striving   perfecting

One of two types of protector parts in your soul that work to extinguish pain. Rather than trying to prevent pain, as managers do, firefighters kick in after a painful event occurs.

Activities include:

overeating   self-harming
addictions   daydreaming
overspending   lashing out

Managers

Firefighters

Spirit-led self
Your self led by the Spirit of God.

creativity   curiosity
clarity   compassion
confidence

Exiles

The vulnerable parts of your soul that you try to push away. Exiles are often stuck in the past, where they hold on to painful memories.

Feelings include:

shame   insecurity   loneliness
fear   hurt   sadness

EXERCISE: THE FIVE STEPS

How to Take a You-Turn When You're Overwhelmed by an Emotion

You may want to find a trusted friend, mentor, spiritual director, or professional counselor to journey with you as you embark on the Five Steps. Even Jesus asked his friends for help when he felt overwhelmed by his emotions (Matt. 26:36–38). This work is a process and not a onetime event. Repeat this exercise anytime a feeling starts to overwhelm you.

What's an emotion you're experiencing right now?

1. **Focus**
   - Where do you sense the feeling physically?
   - Is there a thought or image that comes to mind when you focus on it?
   - How far away from you is it?
   - What is an early memory of this feeling?
2. **Befriend**
   - How do you feel toward this part of your soul?
   - If you feel anything other than curiosity or compassion toward this emotion, notice that part of you and ask it to step back.

- Returning to the part of you that's experiencing the original emotion: Can you extend compassion to this part?
- Is there more it wants you to know?

3. **Invite**
   - Would this part like to invite Jesus to be near?
   - If not, what are its fears and concerns? Can it tell those things to Jesus?
   - Ask Jesus if he wants to say or do anything, or to give you a specific gift.

4. **Unburden**
   - What burden has this part been carrying?
   - Does it have any fears about giving up that burden?
   - Now, how does this part want to release its burden?
   - Does this part want anything in exchange, such as peace, security, or the assurance of love?

5. **Integrate**
   - Check in with any part of you that didn't like your original emotion.
   - What new roles do these two parts want to play in your internal family?
   - Are they willing to be on the same team?
   - Thank them and God for showing up for you today.
   - After you've completed the Five Steps, set an intention to check back in with these parts.

GLOSSARY

Befriend: the second step in the Five Steps of taking a You-Turn. To befriend a part, your Spirit-led self extends curiosity and compassion to a part of your soul and offers the part the care it needs.

Boundaries:

> **External:** lines—physical or imagined—that show where your legitimate sphere of influence and responsibility begins and ends. Typically, boundaries are considered in relation to people and external circumstances.

> **Internal:** imaginary lines that delineate the legitimate sphere of influence and responsibility of the various parts of your soul. Just as you can set boundaries with other people, so you can set boundaries with your own thoughts and feelings.

> **Healthy:** clarity and harmony among the various parts of your soul, such that each part understands its sphere of influence and responsibility and executes its role in a valuable, life-giving way.

Burdens: the extreme beliefs, feelings, or memories that parts of your soul take on as a result of painful experiences. You can develop burdens anytime, but many of them were developed in childhood when your mind couldn't process complex experiences.

Christian: individuals who believe in and follow the teachings of Jesus Christ by accepting his gracious offer of forgiveness and living a life of devotion to him. (See John 1:12; 3:16; Rom. 10:9; Eph. 2:8.)

Comfortable Distance: the outcome of maintaining healthy boundaries with the parts that compete for power inside your soul. Being too close to a troubled part leads to feeling stuck, overwhelmed, and lacking perspective. Being too far from a troubled part leads to being vulnerable to the part ambushing as it seeks to take over the soul. Being at a comfortable distance leads to a sense of lightness and peace.

Constellations (of parts): closely aligned groups of parts within your soul. Parts never exist in isolation, but in interrelated groups. Therefore, when you notice one troubling part, you'll discover that other parts are present.

Creating Space: the act of the Spirit-led self asking a troubled part of the soul to relax, step back, and allow for the self to lead, and perhaps for another part to express itself. When a part steps back, you're able to get to know it better.

Differentiation: the process of distinguishing between two or more things. You differentiate internally when you choose to create more space between your Spirit-led self and the various parts of your soul. As you differentiate from these parts, you can begin to see them with the compassion of your Spirit-led self.

Exiles: vulnerable parts of your soul that harbor fear, guilt, shame, grief, loneliness, insecurities, and other painful emotions. You might need to ask your exiles to step back or to come closer so you can give them the care they need. Exiles are often stuck in the past, where they hold on to painful memories.

Firefighters: one of two types of "protector" parts in your soul (see also *managers*) that work to extinguish the pain of overwhelming thoughts and feelings. Rather than trying to *prevent* pain, as managers do, firefighters kick in *after* a painful event occurs by indulging excessively in distracting, feel-good behavior. Because you can't numb selectively, when firefighters numb your pain, they numb your joy as well.

Five Steps, the: an effective approach to setting healthy boundaries with your soul's troubling thoughts and feelings, so that members of your internal family can coexist harmoniously. A simplified and Christ-centered approach to the IFS therapy model, the Five Steps are:

Step 1: **Focus** on an overwhelming part of yourself.
Step 2: **Befriend** this part you don't like.
Step 3: **Invite** Jesus to draw near.
Step 4: **Unburden** this weary part.
Step 5: **Integrate** it into your internal team of rivals.

Focus: the first step in the Five Steps of taking a You-Turn. To focus, become curious about the strongest thought or feeling you're experiencing. You might notice where in your body you sense that part manifesting itself. In addition, you might use your God-given imagination to envision the part. Then notice what other thoughts or feelings you have toward the part, and ask these other parts to step back so you can focus on the original part with curiosity and compassion.

Holy Spirit: according to Christian tradition, the third person in the Trinity is a divine person who possesses a mind, a will, and emotions. The Spirit serves as comforter and counselor to Christians. (See the book of Acts for more on the Holy Spirit, as well as Ps. 139:7–8; John 14; Rom. 8:26–27; 1 Cor. 2:10–11; and Eph. 4:30.)

Integrate: the fifth step in the Five Steps of taking a You-Turn. Integration occurs as your Spirit-led self guides opposing factions within your soul to reconcile. To integrate, you negotiate with conflicting parts of yourself setting boundaries that support your life's values, vision, mission, and goals. Integration achieves harmony among the once-adversarial parts of your internal family.

Internal Allies: parts of your soul—former rivals—that have worked through the Five Steps and thus have begun operating collaboratively and constructively. Internal enemies transform into allies once troublesome parts take on new, more helpful roles. (See also *team of rivals*.)

Internal Enemies: unruly parts of your soul that you don't like and that battle with other parts for control of your internal family. Internal enemies are either too far from or too close to your Spirit-led self.

Internal Family: your soul's parts, plus your Spirit-led self. These parts relate to one another much like members of a biological family—some members get along well, and others do not. Members of your internal family need to know their roles and need the leadership of your Spirit-led self in order for you to experience inner harmony. In this book, *internal family* is a synonym for *soul*. It's not possible or necessary to know how many parts you have, but it's helpful to get to know the ones most familiar to you.

Internal Family Systems Model of Therapy (IFS): a fast-growing, evidence-based model of psychotherapy developed by psychologist Richard C. Schwartz. The IFS model helps individuals to work with the different, competing parts of themselves for the purpose of freeing parts from their extreme roles, restoring trust in the "Self," and leading the various parts so they can work together harmoniously.[1]

Invite: the third step in the Five Steps of taking a You-Turn. Inviting occurs when you welcome parts of your soul into closer relationship with Jesus. Typically, this occurs when you ask the part if it would like him to draw near.

Legacy Burdens: a type of burden attained through your family or the culture in which you were raised.

Managers: one of two types of "protector" parts in your soul (see also *firefighters*) that attempt to keep you safe emotionally and help you cope. They're called managers because they keep you moving forward by driving you to perform, produce, protect, and please. Managers have a survival instinct and believe it's impractical for you to get bogged down with pain. At their worst, if not kept within healthy boundary lines, they can keep you from experiencing deep-down joy and genuine connection with others.

Overwhelm: an unpleasant, unnecessarily extreme experience triggered when an exile doesn't receive the care it needs from your Spirit-led self and floods your soul. In this book, for simplicity, the word also refers to times a protector takes over, or eclipses, the Spirit-led self. For this concept, Internal Family Systems uses the term *blended* and psychology more broadly uses the term *enmeshed*.

Parts: a term used in Internal Family Systems (IFS) therapy to refer to the various aspects, or states, of the human soul. Parts have their own distinct thoughts, feelings, and character traits. Each part also carries its own story—a narrative about its role. Parts develop as you grow up, and they become problematic when they're hurt or traumatized. Ultimately, the goal is not to get rid of your soul's parts (which would be impossible), but rather, to help them heal and be restored to their valuable states so they can work collaboratively. (See also *comfortable distance*.)

Parts Detective: an imaginary part of you that personifies your ability to detect the protective or exiled parts of other people. Employing your imaginary parts detective helps you notice, and extend curiosity and compassion, when another person's protective or exiled parts may be driving his or her unhelpful behavior.

Polarized/Polarization: an internal state in which two parts "relate in opposition to or in competition with each other, to the point where each party's access to the self is constrained by fear that the other party will win or take over."[2] Polarization leads to division and conflict.

Protectors: types of parts that attempt to protect exiled parts from feeling pain. There are two kinds of protector parts: managers and firefighters.

Quest for Redemption: a subconscious effort to re-create a situation in which you were wounded so that the wounded part of yourself can find healing or grow in some way.

Self: the IFS term for your soul at its purest—the essential you—which provides leadership and has healing qualities, such as compassion, perspective, curiosity, and confidence.

Sin: missing the mark and falling short of God's perfect, holy standards. "For all have sinned and fall short of the glory of God, and all are justified freely by his grace through the redemption that came by Christ Jesus" (Rom. 3:23–24). When parts are hurt or traumatized, they get forced into extreme thoughts, feelings, and roles and become more susceptible to sin.

Soul: the nonphysical part of who you are, composed of your mind, will, and emotions. Used interchangeably in this book with *internal family*.

Speaking on Behalf of a Part: setting a gentle boundary with an agitated part of your soul and sharing with others how you're feeling, without doing harm. For example, when you speak *from* your anger, you might say, "I hate you!" In contrast, when you speak *on behalf of* your anger, you're able to say, "I appreciate you, and a part of me is feeling angry right now."

Spirit-Led Self: the term used in this book for your self led by the Spirit of God. From your Spirit-led self, you can be attuned to your troubling thoughts and emotions and give them the care they need. The Spirit-led self is not a part; rather, it is the core of who you are. Its role is to lead the parts of your soul like a symphony conductor so that they can work harmoniously.

Spirit-Led Self-Leadership: a counseling approach created by the authors that integrates boundaries concepts with the Internal Family Systems (IFS) model of therapy viewed through a Christian lens. The process leads hurting parts of your soul into fellowship with God, resulting in healthy boundaries within your soul. The hallmark of Spirit-led self-leadership is a soul that is calm, caring, curious, compassionate, confident, connected, creative, courageous, and clear, and which exhibits the fruit of the Spirit (found in Galatians 5).[3]

Take Over: an unhelpful experience of a protector part of your soul exerting too much influence. This problem occurs when a protector is not working in partnership with the Spirit-led self.

Team of Rivals: polarized parts of your internal family that, after working through the Five Steps, begin operating collaboratively with the leadership of your Spirit-led self. The term is also the title of a book about President Abraham Lincoln by Doris Kearns Goodwin.

Theology Inspector: an imaginary part that personifies your ability to detect theological inaccuracies. Deploying your imaginary theology inspector helps you notice when someone is making claims that contradict scriptural truths.

Unburden: the fourth step in the Five Steps of taking a You-Turn. Unburdening occurs as you invite an exiled part of yourself to cast off its burdens. Parts that have been stuck in the past can be updated and retrieved from the past, joining your Spirit-led self in the present.

Update: what happens when the Spirit-led self informs an exile of all the strengths, resources, and wisdom your internal family has gained over the years since the exile became stuck due to painful circumstances.

You-Turn: a term representing the process of looking within to bring overwhelming parts of your soul under the leadership of your Spirit-led self.[4] Taking a You-Turn helps you speak with intentionality and care instead of reacting to or avoiding a difficult situation. It also helps you move from seeing your thoughts and feelings as the problem to seeing them as part of the solution.

ACKNOWLEDGMENTS

LEARNING HAPPENS IN community, so it is with deepest gratitude that we extend our heartfelt thanks:

To our friends, mentors, professors, and trainers who encouraged us in this project at important moments. John Townsend, who believed in us and our vision from the very beginning. Dick Schwartz and the Internal Family Systems (IFS) community. The Imago trainers and colleagues who taught us many of the helpful principles interwoven in these pages. Our encouraging agent Wes Yoder and our adept marketing consultant Rob Eagar. Jenny Baumgartner and the amazing Thomas Nelson publishing family. Christians in the Visual Arts who first invited us to teach these concepts. Each of you believed in this message and took a chance so that it might find its way to the public.

To the wise and winsome Elizabeth Cunningham, for your help with editing. To all the people who read and made suggestions for the manuscript and encouraged us along the way. To our clients, whose courageous journeys have informed this work. And to those clients who allowed us to share elements of their stories throughout this book (with the assurance that details have been changed to protect their identities).

From Kim:

To my dear friend, Alison, who first had the idea to write a book together! Your enthusiasm for life and ministry never fails to encourage me. To my wonderful family, especially to my parents and role models, Harville Hendrix and Helen LaKelly Hunt, for loving me and lifting up my voice. To my uncle, Ray Hunt, and my Texas family, whom I love and admire so much. To my aunt, June Hunt, for exemplifying a life fully sold out for Jesus Christ. To my aunt, Swanee Hunt, who helped me hone my craft as a writer and who generously opened her home for many writing retreats. To Melia, Hunter, Leah, and Ron; to my big sister, Kathryn Ruth, who received the Heart Award from her classmates in high school and who wins it again and again, every day, in my eyes. To my beloved husband, Ken, a gifted teacher and author, for reading every page, for offering steady wisdom, and for helping with the King David story in the introduction, as well as the Lincoln section in chapter 8. The goodness that can be found in these pages I witness daily in your life.

From Alison:

To my coauthor extraordinaire, Kim, who first introduced me to the concepts of IFS. It has been an honor to take this journey with you. To my sister, Courtney, whose artistic sensibility and knack for words have shaped my heart and soul from the beginning. Thank you for lending your time, talent, and listening ear throughout this project. To my mom and dad, Willard and Sally Cook, your example of faithful, persistent love and service is an inspiration. To John and Veronica, I am ever grateful for the joy you always bring. To Judy and David, your back porch is a writer's dream— thank you. To Gary and Nancy, the influence of your wisdom is woven throughout these pages. To Brooke and Chase, your astute observations and good humor made this project possible, and you encourage me daily with your example of tenacity. Best of all, your love for the Wyoming mountains brought me home. And to my husband, Joe, whose support for, and belief in, me has been unfailing. Your ability to bring clarity and perspective is a gift from heaven—it has been my greatest joy to become one with you.

And we give praise to the triune God of grace, for being ever near:

> May [I] be found in Him, not having a righteousness of my own derived from the Law, but that which is through faith in Christ, the righteousness which comes from God on the basis of faith, that I may know Him and the power of His resurrection and the fellowship of His sufferings, being conformed to His death; in order that I may attain to the resurrection from the dead. Not that I have already obtained it or have already become perfect, but I press on so that I may lay hold of that for which also I was laid hold of by Christ Jesus. . . . I do not regard myself as having laid hold of it yet; but one thing I do: forgetting what lies behind and reaching forward to what lies ahead, I press on toward the goal for the prize of the upward call of God in Christ Jesus.
>
> —PHILIPPIANS 3:9–14 NASB

ABOUT THE AUTHORS

Alison Cook, MA, PhD, practices in the greater Boston area, where she specializes in the integration of spiritual formation and psychology. She has taught and counseled teens, adults, and couples for over two decades and speaks on emotional and spiritual wholeness at churches, conferences, and retreats across the country.

Originally from Wyoming, Alison studied at Dartmouth College before returning West to earn an MA in counseling from Denver Seminary and a PhD in religion and psychology from the University of Denver. Her doctoral dissertation was on the relationship between religion and prejudice, and as a result of her work she co-founded a non-profit tutoring company to help bring affordable tutoring to underserved students. She is certified in Internal Family Systems Therapy.

Alison, her husband, Joe, and their two teens are active in the ministry of the Salvation Army and enjoy hiking and back-packing as often as they can.

Connect with Alison on her website at:
www.alisoncookphd.com.

Kimberly Miller, MTh, LMFT, is a licensed marriage and family therapist in private practice, specializing in prevent-ing burnout among leaders. Kim is the founder of Leading

Wholeheartedly, a ministry equipping people to cultivate their inner lives so that their service to others is more deeply rooted, productive, and sustainable. She also founded Doing Good Well, a program of Christians in the Visual Arts. Prior to working as a counselor, Kim served as a campus minister with InterVarsity Christian Fellowship at Harvard University.

Kim studied religion at Davidson College, earned a master's in theology from Regent College, and an MA in clinical psychology from Azusa Pacific University. She is certified in Internal Family Systems Therapy and Imago Relationship Therapy.

A Dallas native, Kim and her husband, Ken, enjoy gardening, spending time with friends and family, and extending hospitality at their southern California home.

Connect with Kim on her website at:
www.kimberlyjunemiller.com.

NOTES

INTRODUCTION

1. 2 Sam. 11:3.
2. Henry Cloud and John Townsend, *Boundaries: When to Say Yes, How to Say No to Take Control of Your Life* (Grand Rapids: Zondervan, 1992), 245–46.
3. For a useful summary of this model, see "Evolution of the Internal Family Systems Model by Dr. Richard Schwartz, Ph.D.," Center for Self-Leadership, accessed September 21, 2017, https://selfleadership.org/about-internal-family-systems.html.
4. The Internal Family Systems (IFS) therapy model is acknowledged as "evidence-based" by the National Registry for Evidence-Based Programs and Practices. For more information, see "IFS, an Evidence-Based Practice," Foundation News, Foundation for Self-Leadership, accessed September 29, 2017, http://www.foundationifs.org/news-articles/79-ifs-an-evidence-based-practice. The authors have condensed the model and adapted it from a Christian worldview.
5. Dallas Willard, *Renovation of the Heart: Putting on the Character of Christ* (Colorado Springs: NavPress, 2002), 27.

CHAPTER 1: WHY BOUNDARIES FOR YOUR SOUL?

1. Dictionary.com, s.v. "soul," accessed August 21, 2017, http://www.dictionary.com/browse/soul?s=t.
2. Willard, *Renovation of the Heart*, 37 (see intro., n. 5).
3. Dictionary.com, s.v. "boundary," accessed August 21, 2017, http://www.dictionary.com/browse/boundary?s=t.
4. Harville Hendrix and Helen LaKelly Hunt, *Making Marriage Simple: 10 Truths for Changing the Relationship You Have into the One You Want* (New York: Harmony, 2013), 37.

5. We explore the term *team of rivals* in chapter 8.

6. Ask a Librarian, Harvard Law School Library online, accessed August 21, 2017, http://asklib.law.harvard.edu/faq/115309. Since the late 1930s, every year at commencement, the Harvard University president says to Harvard Law School graduates the following phrase, coined by professor John MacArthur Maguire (1924–1973): "You are now ready to aid in the shaping and application of those wise restraints that make men free."

7. These You-Turn steps are based on the Internal Family Systems (IFS) therapy model, which, as noted earlier, is acknowledged as "evidence-based" by the National Registry for Evidence-based Programs and Practices (see intro., n. 4).

8. From the subtitle of Cloud and Townsend, *Boundaries* (see intro., n. 2).

CHAPTER 2: YOUR SPIRIT-LED SELF

1. Henri J. M. Nouwen, *The Inner Voice of Love: A Journey Through Anguish to Freedom*, repr. ed. (New York: Image, 1998), 14.

2. Cloud and Townsend, *Boundaries*, 46 (see intro., n. 2).

3. Richard C. Schwartz, *Introduction to the Internal Family Systems Model* (Oak Park, IL: Trailhead, 2001), 33–48.

4. *Spirit-led self-leadership* is a term we created. It is adapted from the term *self-leadership*, which is used in the Internal Family Systems therapy model. See Schwartz, 30–54.

5. For more on this topic, see C. S. Lewis, *The Screwtape Letters: How a Senior Devil Instructs a Junior Devil in the Art of Temptation* (New York: Time, 1961); and Dallas Willard, *Hearing God* (Downers Grove, IL: InterVarsity Press, 2012).

6. Willard, *Renovation of the Heart*, 27 (see intro., n. 5).

CHAPTER 3: THREE PARTS OF YOU

1. Curt Thompson, in discussion with Kimberly Miller, April 10, 2015.

2. For more on the IFS model, see Schwartz, *Introduction to the Internal Family Systems Model*, 55–88 (see chap. 2, n. 3).

3. For more on the soul's three kinds of parts, see Schwartz, *Introduction to the Internal Family Systems Model*, 89–121 (see chap. 2, n. 3).

4. From the title of the popular 1980s song written by Jim Steinman and made popular by Welsh vocalist Bonnie Tyler.

5. Schwartz, *Introduction to the Internal Family Systems Model*, 90 (see chap. 2, n. 3).

6. L. Y. Abramson, M. E. Seligman, and J. D. Teasdale, "Learned

Helplessness in Humans: Critique and Reformulation," *Journal of Abnormal Psychology* 87, no. 1 (1978): 49–74.

7. Andy Crouch, *Strong and Weak: Embracing a Life of Love, Risk, and True Flourishing* (Downers Grove, IL: InterVarsity Press, 2016), 11.

8. "August 15, 2013—The results from a randomized controlled study, published in the *Journal of Rheumatology*, show that an IFS-based intervention had positive effects on patients with Rheumatoid Arthritis (RA), reducing pain and depressive symptoms, while improving physical function and self-compassion. . . . Dr. Nancy Shadick, from the Department of Medicine at Brigham and Women's Hospital at Harvard Medical School, served as Principal Investigator for the study, which assessed the impact of an IFS-based psychotherapeutic intervention on disease activity and psychological status in a trial of 79 RA patients. The study concluded that IFS is feasible and acceptable for patients with RA and would effectively complement medical management of the disease." "IFS Shown to Reduce Pain and Depression, and Improve Physical Function for Rheumatoid Arthritis Patients," Center for Self Leadership, August 15, 2013, https://selfleadership.org/ifs-rheumatology-study .html.

CHAPTER 4: STEP ONE: FOCUS

1. For a discussion of what IFS calls "clusters" of parts, see Schwartz, *Introduction to the Internal Family Systems Model*, 67–73 (see chap. 2, n. 3).

2. Anne Lamott, *Bird by Bird: Some Instructions on Writing and Life* (New York: Anchor, 1995), 27.

3. Teresa of Ávila, *The Interior Castle*, trans. E. Allison Peers, (n.p.: Dover, 2007), 15, quoting John 14:2, "In my Father's house there are many mansions" (KJV).

4. See, for example, "Dr. Dan Siegel on Neuroplasticity: An Excerpt from Mind," PsychAlive, accessed September 19, 2017, https://www .psychalive.org/dr-daniel-siegel-neuroplasticity/.

5. Alexis de Tocqueville, *Democracy in America* (New York: Alfred A. Knopf, 1994), 563.

CHAPTER 5: STEP TWO: BEFRIEND

1. Henri Nouwen, *Reaching Out: The Three Movements of the Spiritual Life* (New York: Doubleday, 1975), 71.

2. Toni Herbine Blank, Internal Family Systems "Online Circle"

training video, 10:00, accessed December 12, 2017, https://ifscircle
.com.

CHAPTER 6: STEP THREE: INVITE

1. Brother Lawrence, *The Practice of the Presence of God*, rev. ed. (New Kensington, PA: Whitaker House, 1982), 26.
2. Marjorie J. Thompson, *Soul Feast: An Invitation to the Christian Spiritual Life* (Louisville, KY: Westminster John Knox, 1995), 7.
3. Richard J. Foster, *Celebration of Discipline: The Path to Spiritual Growth*, 3rd ed. (New York: HarperCollins, 1998), 7.

CHAPTER 7: STEP FOUR: UNBURDEN

1. Bessel van der Kolk, *The Body Keeps the Score*, 1 (see chap. 3, n. 3).
2. Richard C. Schwartz, *Internal Family Systems Therapy* (New York: Guilford, 1994), 138.
3. Richard Rohr and Andreas Ebert, *The Enneagram: A Christian Perspective* (New York: Crossroad, 2004), 54.
4. For more on attempts to re-create childhood relational dynamics in hopes of redeeming the past, see Harville Hendrix, *Getting the Love You Want: A Guide for Couples* (New York: Henry Holt, 2008), 34–44.
5. Nouwen, *The Inner Voice of Love*, 49 (see chap. 2, n. 1).
6. Schwartz, *Internal Family Systems Therapy*, 98–99.
7. Gal. 6:5; Cloud and Townsend, *Boundaries*, 30–31 (see intro., n. 2).
8. For more on passive rescue wishes, see John Townsend, *The Entitlement Cure: Finding Success in Doing Hard Things the Right Way* (Grand Rapids: Zondervan, 2015), 268.
9. Schwartz, *Introduction to the Internal Family Systems Model*, 33–48 (see chap. 2, n. 3).
10. Howard Thurman, *Disciplines of the Spirit* (New York: Harper & Row, 1963), 108.

CHAPTER 8: STEP FIVE: INTEGRATE

1. Abraham Lincoln, *The Collected Works of Abraham Lincoln*, ed. Roy P. Basler, vol. 2 (New Brunswick, NJ: Rutgers University Press, 1953), 461.
2. Doris Kearns Goodwin, *Team of Rivals: The Political Genius of Abraham Lincoln* (New York: Simon & Schuster, 2005).
3. Abraham Lincoln, *The Collected Works of Abraham Lincoln*, ed. Roy P. Basler, vol. 8 (New Brunswick, NJ: Rutgers University Press, 1953), 332.

4. Schwartz, *Introduction to the Internal Family Systems Model*, 144 (see chap. 2, n. 3).
5. Abraham Lincoln, first inaugural address, in *The Collected Works of Abraham Lincoln*, ed. Roy P. Basler, vol. 4 (Rockville, MD: Wildside, 2008), 271.
6. Helen LaKelly Hunt, *Faith and Feminism: A Holy Alliance* (New York: Atria, 2004), 53.
7. Frederick Buechner, *Wishful Thinking—A Theological ABC by Frederick Buechner* (New York: Harper & Row, 1973), 95.
8. Kim learned of this exercise from Betsy McConnell, who said she was inspired by Richard Schwartz.

CHAPTER 9: BOUNDARIES WITH ANGER

1. *English Oxford Dictionaries*, s.v. "anger," accessed September 22, 2017, https://en.oxforddictionaries.com/definition/anger.
2. June Hunt, *How to Forgive When You Don't Feel Like It* (Eugene, OR: Harvest House, 2007), 211–12.
3. *Mayim* in Hebrew is the word used here for *waters*. See the use of *waters* in Jonah 2:5: "The engulfing waters threatened me, the deep surrounded me." *Ellicott's Commentary for English Readers* says, "The figure of overwhelming waters is a common one in Hebrew song to represent some crushing sorrow." "Jonah 2:5," Bible Hub, accessed December 13, 2017, http://biblehub.com/commentaries/jonah/2-5.htm.
4. Schwartz, *Introduction to the Internal Family Systems Model*, 120 (see chap. 2, n. 3).
5. Catharina von Schlegel, "Be Still, My Soul," *Lutheran Worship* (St. Louis, MO: Concordia, 1986).

CHAPTER 10: BOUNDARIES WITH FEAR AND ANXIETY

1. *English Oxford Dictionaries*, s.v. "fear," accessed September 22, 2017, https://en.oxforddictionaries.com/definition/fear.
2. *English Oxford Dictionaries*, s.v. "anxiety," accessed September 22, 2017, https://en.oxforddictionaries.com/definition/anxiety.
3. Mother Teresa, *Come Be My Light: The Private Writings of the Saint of Calcutta* (New York: Doubleday, 2007), 187.
4. Mother Teresa, *Come Be My Light*, 188.
5. C. S. Lewis, *The Screwtape Letters and Screwtape Proposes a Toast* (New York: Macmillan, 1961), 39.
6. Mary Oliver, "The Summer Day," *New and Selected Poems*, vol. 1 (Boston: Beacon, 1992), 94.

NOTES

CHAPTER 11: BOUNDARIES WITH SADNESS

1. *Dictionary.com*, s.v. "sad," accessed September 22, 2017, http://www .dictionary.com/browse/sad?s=t.
2. Henri J. M. Nouwen, *Life of the Beloved: Spiritual Living in a Secular World* (New York: Crossroad, 1992), 92.
3. These three categories are from The Goodbye Process exercise, developed by Harville Hendrix, which Kim learned from personal communication with him.
4. Miranda Lambert, "The House That Built Me," by Tom Douglas and Allen Shamblin, MP3, on *Revolution*, Columbia Nashville, 2009.
5. Joni Eareckson Tada, "December 27: Inward Pain," *More Precious Than Silver: 366 Daily Devotional Readings* (Grand Rapids: Zondervan, 1998), 393.

CHAPTER 12: BOUNDARIES WITH ENVY AND DESIRE

1. *Merriam-Webster Dictionary*, s.v. "envy," accessed September 25, 2017, https://www.merriam-webster.com/dictionary/envy.
2. *English Oxford Dictionaries*, s.v. "desire," accessed September 25, 2017, https://en.oxforddictionaries.com/definition/desire.
3. See the usage note for "jealous," accessed September 19, 2017, The Free Dictionary by Farlex, http://www.thefreedictionary.com/jealous.
4. Examples include: Deuteronomy 32:16; Joshua 24:19; Psalm 78:58.
5. Schwartz, *Introduction to the Internal Family Systems Model*, 119 (see chap. 2, n. 3).
6. C. S. Lewis, *The Weight of Glory: And Other Addresses* (New York: HarperOne, 1949), 25–26.

CHAPTER 13: BOUNDARIES WITH GUILT AND SHAME

1. The Free Dictionary by Farlex, s.v., "guilt," accessed September 25, 2017, http://www.thefreedictionary.com/guilt.
2. The Free Dictionary by Farlex, s.v. "shame," accessed September 25, 2017, http://www.thefreedictionary.com/shame.
3. June Hunt, *Counseling Through Your Bible Handbook* (Eugene, OR: Harvest House, 2008), 19.
4. Madeleine L'Engle, *Two-Part Invention: The Story of a Marriage* (New York: HarperCollins, 1988).
5. Brené Brown, "The Power of Vulnerability," YouTube video, 20:49, posted by TED, January 3, 2011, https://www.youtube.com /watch?v=iCvmsMzlF7o.

6. Curt Thompson, *The Soul of Shame: Retelling the Stories We Believe About Ourselves* (Downers Grove, IL: InterVarsity, 2015), 34.
7. Thompson, *The Soul of Shame*, 12.
8. Curt Thompson, *Anatomy of the Soul* (Carol Stream, IL: Tyndale, 2010), 53.

CHAPTER 14: BOUNDARIES WITH CHALLENGING PARTS OF OTHERS

1. Wayne Muller, *Sabbath: Finding Rest, Renewal, and Delight in Our Busy Lives* (New York: Bantam, 1999), 183.
2. Brené Brown, *The Gifts of Imperfection* (Center City, MN: Hazelden, 2010), 61.
3. Dan Siegel, *Mindsight: The New Science of Personal Transformation* (New York: Bantam, 2010), 116.
4. Thompson, *Anatomy of the Soul*, 3–4 (see chap. 13, n. 8).
5. N. T. Wright, *Evil and the Justice of God* (Downers Grove, IL: InterVarsity Press, 2006), 145.
6. All of these statements are drawn from the Bible and are listed in the book by June Hunt, *Seeing Yourself Through God's Eyes* (Eugene, OR: Harvest House, 2008).

GLOSSARY

1. Center for Self Leadership, accessed October 2, 2017, https://www.selfleadership.org/.
2. Schwartz, *Introduction to the Internal Family Systems Model*, 144 (see chap. 2, n. 3).
3. IFS uses the term *Self-leadership*.
4. IFS uses the term *U-Turn* in the same way.